Adrian Clarke

Rachel Cusk was born in 1967. She is the author of the memoir *A Life's Work: On Becoming a Mother* and of seven novels: *Saving Agnes,* which won the Whitbread First Novel Award; *The Temporary; The Country Life,* which won the Somerset Maugham Award; *The Lucky Ones,* which was shortlisted for the Whitbread Novel Award; *In the Fold; Arlington Park,* which was shortlisted for the Orange Broadband Prize for Fiction; and *The Bradshaw Variations.* In 2003, Cusk was chosen as one of *Granta*'s Best of Young British Novelists. She lives in Brighton, England.

ALSO BY RACHEL CUSK

THE LAST SUPPER

THE LAST SUPPER
A Summer in Italy

∝

RACHEL CUSK

∝

Picador

Farrar, Straus and Giroux   New York

www.picadorusa.com

Picador® is a U.S. registered trademark and is used by Farrar, Straus and Giroux under license from Pan Books Limited.

For information on Picador Reading Group Guides, please contact Picador. E-mail: readinggroupguides@picadorusa.com

Designed by Jonathan D. Lippincott

ISBN 978-0-312-42965-2
ISBN 0-312-42965-7

Originally published in Great Britain by Faber and Faber Limited

First Picador Edition: May 2010

Comes over one an absolute necessity to move. And what is more, to move in some particular direction. A double necessity then: to get on the move, and to know whither.

—D. H. Lawrence, *Sea and Sardinia*

CONTENTS

ILLUSTRATIONS

THE LAST SUPPER

SELF-PORTRAIT, WITH DINOSAURS

At night I would often be woken by noise from the road, and afterward would lie awake for hours, unable to sleep. The noise, which was of a strange drunken revelry, would usually begin long after the pubs had closed, though in the deeps of the night I never knew exactly what time it was. I was merely summoned by the sound of unearthly groans and shrieks outside my window that seemed to belong neither to the world nor to my dreams but somewhere in between. They might have been men's voices or women's, it was hard to tell. The noise they made came from a region that outlay human identity. Their long, inchoate monologues, vocalized yet senseless, seemed to name something that afterward could not be specified, to describe what by daylight appeared indescribable.

This demoniacal groaning would often go on for so long that it seemed impossible it could be coming from living people passing on the pavements. It was the sound of lost souls, of primitive creatures bellowing far inside the earth. Yet I never got up to look: the noise was so unreal that it was only when it stopped that I felt myself to be actually awake. Then I would lie there, full of a feeling of insecurity, as though the world were a wildly spinning fairground ride from which my bed might work loose and be somehow flung away. The groaning sounds and the darkness and

the carelessly spinning earth, offering me its fathomless glimpses
of space, of nothingness: all this would run on for one hour or
two or three, I couldn't tell. The hours were blank and sealed,
filled with gray information: one after another they were dis-
patched.

Then another sound would begin, dimly at first, a kind of
humming or droning, steady and industrious. After a while it filled
the room with its monotonous note. This was the sound of traffic.
People were going in their cars to work. A little later a finger of
wan light showed itself at the curtains. When I was a child the
night seemed as big as an ocean to me, deep and static: you rowed
across it for hour after hour and sometimes got so lost in time and
darkness that it seemed as if the morning might never be found.
Now it was a mere vacuum, filling up with human activity as
a dump is filled with discarded objects. It was an empty space
into which the overcrowded world was extending its outskirts, its
sprawl.

We were living in Bristol at that time, and the slaving past of
the city was always present to me, though in the middle-class dis-
trict of Clifton its brutality was largely semantic, recalling itself
amid the boutiques and sofa shops of Whiteladies Road and
Blackboys Hill. Yet it seemed to have seeped into the masonry, into
the paving stones. I was often told that the beautiful Georgian
terraces of Clifton had for years been neglected and threatened
with demolition and that students and artists had lived there con-
tentedly in conditions approximating squalor. But that was in the
past: these days the slave owners' houses were smart again and
unaffordable, the streets lined with beauty salons and expensive
cars, the baize lawns of the private schools trodden by millionaires' children from China, America, Japan. Clifton estate agents
carried themselves with the preening significance of royal cour-

tiers, while the fume-throttled city sprawled below, with its bombed-out center, its ghettos, its miles of strange, impoverished housing, its uneasy atmosphere both of misrule and of a thorough-minded, inexorable division.

Something of the hard-heartedness of that imperial past seemed to live on in the people I met and spoke to every day. Man, woman, and child, they found sensitivity intolerable. Nothing irked them more than the liberal conscience, unless it was an outspoken sense of injustice. These things impinged on their free bigotry, and on the sense of humor that depended on it. They were not cold or unfriendly; quite the reverse. It was just that their philosophy formed an edifice of startling indelicacy amid the fluted columns and porticoes, the classical perspectives and cloudlike silhouettes, the ancient parks and pavilions, the secret rotundas and rich, ornamented interiors that were their habitat. It was a philosophy composed of two primitive blocks: that everyone should work for what he had; and that what mattered were the good things in life.

Encompassing so little in and of itself, this was a philosophy that required, for the sake of texture, of content, a God—and indeed the churches of Clifton did a thriving trade, on the import and the export side alike. I encountered notions of Christian charity that might have come from the pages of a Victorian novel, so ignorant did they seem of the concept of social democracy, and was beleaguered everywhere by advertisements for the evangelical Alpha course, which, for an initiative that targets those who have lost their way in life, seemed in Clifton to be remarkably well attended. These advertisements took a somewhat startling form: one day I passed one and was driven to stop and look at it twice. It was a photograph of a man in climbing equipment standing in sunlight on the pinnacle of a mountain. I was surprised, almost affronted, by the caption, which read: *Is there more to life than this?* I wasn't entirely sure there was, nor ought to be. But I pondered it all the same. It had a profound effect on me, though not quite the one it intended. Whenever I thought of it, I felt myself drawing to the threshold of a revelation, a realization so large that it was difficult to see its full extent.

Down in the city, the turgid river creeps between its sludge-gray banks. The Avon Gorge rises steeply to either side. A busy road runs down it: the roar of traffic echoes all along the chasm, rising and revolving like a vortex. Once there were mammoths here, and bears, and strange swimming dinosaurs with pointed beaks and close-set eyes. There is a placard by the gorge with drawings of these creatures, and a timeline. It is as straight as a ruler: it runs through the Paleolithic and the Neolithic and the Jurassic, through ice ages colored blue. At the end there is the stub of humanity, smaller than an arrowhead on its long shaft of time. Where it is going nobody knows. The line stops: the future is blank.

Every day at the same time I leave the house and walk my children to school. They are five and six. They each wear a navy-blue uniform, and carry a nylon schoolbag of the same color. These things identify them, just as in their picture books the Romans are identified by their togas, the Victorians by their bustles and top hats. They are modern schoolchildren: they belong to their moment in history, which gathers them up in its great impersonal wave. Now and then they make a toga out of a sheet, or dress up in the crumpled raiment of an Indian squaw that lies with other costumes in a chest in their room. In the dim light of an English winter in an English provincial city, the forms of other eras vaguely suggest themselves, like mountains in mist. But none of it obstructs the passage of the arrow that flies on and on into its endlessly repeating blankness. They go to school and come back again, go and come back, go and come back. They are happy enough to do it, though they retain a certain neutrality, as though they have been promised an explanation and are patiently waiting for it to be given.

It is on their behalf that I nurture my deepest stores of repulsion for the God advertisement and its insolent question. If there are to be lies, let them not concern the value of life, for not everyone has tired of it yet. Let them not denigrate the world, for there are those whose chance to see it has not yet come.

∝

On New Year's Eve we go to a party on Dartmoor. In the morning I wake in an unfamiliar bedroom and look through the window at the moor veiled with rain. The shrouded hills are desolate. They seem to extend on and on, into an indistinct kind of infinity. After breakfast the women sit on sofas, talking. Their children dart in and out. Sometimes they reach out and catch one, to hold its squirming body and stroke its bright, fine hair. Their female forms are fixed and sculptural: though the children squirm, they are glad to be held by something so firm. The women are both shelter and shrine—they offer and at the same time they ask. They have agreed to stay still: it is the children who choose, between security and risk. It is important that they choose correctly. They mustn't cling to their mothers; nor must they forget to swim past, close enough to be caught.

I stare through the window. From here it looks as though you could walk into the vista of gray hills and never stop, walk and walk without ever reaching anything you could call by its name.

∝

In time we decided to leave Clifton and move elsewhere. Our friends were sorry to see us go. They did not believe that we would find a place we liked better, for it seemed obvious to them that we were afflicted with restlessness and with a love of the unknown that in their eyes was a kind of curse, like the curses in mythology that are forever sending people from their homes to seek what perhaps can never be found, for it is in the seeking itself that the punishment lies. Yet I had a terror of my own, which was the fear of knowing something in its entirety. To seek held no particular fear for me: it was to find, and to know, and to come to the end of knowing that I shrank from.

Go we must: go we would. But where? In the novels I read, people were forever disappearing off to Italy at a moment's notice, to wait out unpropitious seasons of life in warm and cultured surroundings. It was a cure for everything: love, disappointment, stupidity, strange vaporous maladies of the lungs. And for disenchantment, too, perhaps; for claustrophobia, and boredom; and for a hunger that seemed to gnaw at the very ligaments of my soul, whose cause was as hidden from me as were the means of its satisfaction.

We decided to go to Italy, though not forever. Three months, a season, was as much of the future as we cared to see. Perhaps we would return to England; perhaps we would not. We put the house on the market and took the children out of their school. To this place, at least, we were never coming back.

∝

The boat we are taking to France leaves from Newhaven, an hour from my parents-in-law's house. The house is in the countryside. Outside, the village lies in ruminative silence. The hills are black and occasionally a cow bellows out of the blackness. We get up while it is still dark; an April darkness, damp, suggestive, faintly hopeful. It is half past four: it is the first stroke of the chisel on the block of our travels, this incision into the night, and the night is resistant. We prize it open, prize the children from their beds, stagger around thick-tongued and white-faced.

My mother-in-law has made breakfast. She moves around downstairs in her dressing gown, perfectly awake and composed. She has a significant air of readiness: she is like a part-time mythical functionary, a night worker, or one of those people in Shakespeare who appear only in the first and last scenes. Her big golden somber-faced dog follows at her heels. She has made porridge, and rolls. The kitchen smells of new bread. There is marmalade to go with the rolls. The dog sighs, turns around, settles down in a heap of golden fur on the red tiles by the hearth. My mother-in-law wishes she were coming with us. Yet just now she is so fixed in her setting, as we have never been: I have never known a place more homelike than this room in the moment before our departure. I imagine us towing the kitchen behind us, with its dog and oak table and eternal porridge pot, across the plains to Florence and Siena.

The two children sit at the table and eat. They keep their rucksacks on while they do it. They do not talk of what it is they are leaving: the unknown has them in its thrall. On their last day of school their classmates presented them with cards and photographs and a present for each of them. When they saw these things, tears of surprise sprang from their eyes. They didn't know they would require mementos. They had never held in their hands things of such finality. Now they say goodbye lavishly to the dog. Do they think they will ever see him again? It's hard to tell. The future is still so incessant to them, coming out of its own blankness in wave after wave and then unexpectedly surfing them back to their own familiar shore. For all they know they might meet him in Italy, sauntering down a street in Rome with his tail wagging in the air, and they'd be more delighted than surprised if they did.

We drive for an hour across the Sussex Downs to Newhaven. For a while it is still dark; then slowly the darkness separates itself from the land. It lifts mysteriously away, leaving everything in a naked blue light. In that blue light England looks like a sleeping baby, looks somehow new and unmarked, with its soft hills and blue-tinted slumbrous fields and distant trees like tiny motionless clouds. Afterward we go along the main road, past Brighton like a bright spill of gems over the hill down to the pale sea, past Lewes, and then we are amid fields again, on the quiet winding road to Newhaven that is like journeying through a painting. I have noticed this before, this road's picturesque aimlessness. It has an abstracted, dreamlike quality. It has a disarming kind of innocence before the thrust of departure, arousing a feeling of love for something already lost, something that perhaps no longer really exists.

∽

At last the blue light resolves itself into the familiar flat gray of an April dawn on the south coast. We wind our way toward the port, past the toylike Parker Pen factory, past the little train station and into the harbor, whose steeply rising grassy sides seem to be undergoing a kind of surgery, with their diggers and their piles of breeze blocks and their half-finished housing developments that look lived in and discarded before they've even been built. Rounding the bend, we see our boat, black plumes of smoke pouring from its funnels, monolithic against the miniature scale of the muddy harbor. There are a few other cars waiting under the gray wadded sky, and some lorries, each like a great beast that has crept out of the night with its solitary driver. It is not yet the holiday season: people are at work; children have returned to school. We stare out of our car windows at the other cars. In the back we have clothes, books, a guitar, a box of toys, tennis rackets, a thermos flask, a large Italian dictionary, a set of watercolors, and a leather-bound backgammon case. Other people seem to have nothing at all. They gaze through their windscreens, their back seats empty. Sometimes there is a pillow in a faded patterned pillowcase lying on the shelf behind, as if it is the only desire they can conceive of feeling, the need to pull up and sleep for an hour or two. We all inch our way gradually forward. I feel as if we are being held in a last moment of compression, like seeds held tightly in a hand before being scattered; as though our obligation to feel connected to others is running down to its last seconds. It is the only thing that remains to be shed, this garment of nationhood. We move slowly forward in the

dull gray light that has broken now over the sea. When it is our
turn we show our passports. We say goodbye to the officer in her
booth, and roll out across the concrete jetty to where the boat
stands shuddering vastly in the water, the smoke streaming from its
chimneys, its doors standing open, its insides showing, its men
amid the ribs in their white overalls, like people in a strange
dream, beckoning us in.

∝

Upstairs the boat smells of baked beans and fried food. I remember this smell from other journeys: it lies just off the shoreline like
an olfactory fence, through which admittance must be gained in or
out. The canteen isn't open yet, but a queue of people is waiting at
the shuttered hatches. We go and sit at the front, in the chilly air-
conditioned salon with its wood veneer and hard gray-upholstered
arrangements of chairs fixed to the floor. When the boat begins to
move we hardly notice. The land slides noiselessly away past the
windows. The gray-blue water churns mildly in front. A few gulls
hover and circle our bulk and eventually drift back to shore.

For a while the two children are excited. They run up and
down the half-empty boat, past people who are sitting silently or
reading newspapers or breaking open packets of food, people who
are conversing brightly despite the early hour, people who are already fathomlessly asleep amid their bags and coats and jackets.
For each of these groups they reserve a measure of interest as they
pass and repass them: they cast out looks as fishermen cast out
lines; they give them an opportunity, an opening. I see that it is, for
them, the central mystery of life, how a course of events forms itself. They tiptoe around the closed bar with its fruit machines pulsing in the shadows. They keep us abreast of developments in the
canteen, which to their satisfaction eventually opens, though this

represents no particular change in their circumstances. For a while they haunt a corner of the salon where a family, all very pale and soft and large and all clad in black, are handing round biscuits and packets of crisps and colorless fizzy lemonade from a plastic liter bottle. The children clearly feel that this is a transaction of which they might at last entertain some hopes. They stay within this family's rustling and torpid aura while the mother glances at them expressionlessly. Finally, they trail back to our table and sit down. They have exhausted every avenue and come back empty-handed. The boat having been found to be a place of no opportunity, they wish to know when we will arrive.

I am studying Italian verbs and phrases. I have a little book in which I write everything down. *Faccio, fai, fa, facciamo, fate, fanno.* I have not yet spoken any of these words: they are a form of trousseau, a virgin's drawerful of unblemished linen. I like them in their spotless condition and cannot quite imagine the congress that is their destiny. *Vengo, vieni, viene, veniamo, venite, vengono.* I also have an Italian textbook, called *Contatti!* There are various recurring characters in *Contatti!*, Italian men consecrated in the national customs of eating and drinking, earnest young Italian women who ask for directions to public landmarks, and even an English couple called the Robinsons. It is full of human situations that are both stilted and consoling, as though through this gauze of language everything impure and uncertain has been filtered away. *The signora arrives with her daughters. The American students work hard. Did you sleep badly at Capodanno?*

It strikes me that *Contatti!* has something about it of Debrett's book of social etiquette, in its insistence on the correct forms of expression within the randomness of the human plight. But there is even more of the atmosphere of the afterlife amid its pages, of an unprogressing limbo where Tony and Mario are forever ordering the appropriate coffee for the time of day at the bar and Marcella, in her loop of eternity, stands on a street corner in Verona asking Fabrizio for directions to the railway station. People are helpful and kind in *Contatti!*, but they are untouched by passion or by failure: they do not scream or cry or love, or try to thwart Peter and Mary Robinson in their ambition to purchase a house in the Italian countryside. *L'agenzia puo fissare una visita al mattino.* The Robinsons seem to have an awful lot of Italian friends for a dull middle-class English couple. They crop up in nearly every chapter, lunching with the Pacianos at their Roman apartment, meeting up for drinks with their old pals Roberto and Carla, Peter banging on all the while about their *casa di campagna*, Mary unfailingly repeating her unatmospheric observation that the Italians don't consume nearly as much alcohol as the English. Because it's *Contatti!*, no one tells them to shut up. *E vero*, says Carla solemnly, *beviano molto poco.* Yet there is something soothing, something almost instructive in their tedium, for *Contatti!* startlingly omits to provide translations for the majority of things I say on a daily basis. I have come to rely on harsh imperatives and interrogatives in verbal expression, though I'm sure this didn't used to be the case. Such grammatical refinements occur much later on in the pages of *Contatti!*, where in all probability I will never find my way. (It is an alleviating prospect, that of being confined to simple statements, straightforward desires, and polite verbal forms.)

The ferry hums in its sphere of gray cloud and water. It is so large that it has encompassed the sensation of travel itself: sealed in and air-conditioned as we are, we appear to be virtually motionless. There is no tipping or rocking, no groaning of timbers, no wind or sea spray on our faces, no work that is necessary to advance us to our destination. There is nothing to do but wait, for one thing to become another. The great gray nothingness inches past the windows. I have the strange feeling that the other passengers are familiar to me. The man with combed-back hair and plaid shirt sitting reading *The Times*, the woman in the Barbour jacket with the face of a withered Memling damsel, the hefty Rhinemaiden doing Sudoku puzzles, who purses her powerful mouth round her pen and scans the air with narrowed eyes— surely I have met them somewhere before. Again and again I look at a face or a hairstyle or even an article of clothing and feel a sense of recognition that is almost like a touching of nerves in distant parts of the body. But instead of gaining substance the feeling recedes and grows indistinct. The memory does not come, just as the memories of certain dreams that on waking seemed so concrete implacably make their way into oblivion, like a train pulling out of a station and slowly vanishing down the tracks.

All the same, it would not surprise me if one of these people came and spoke to me of our shared past, however distant and tangential. In *Contatti!*, Roberto tells the waiter that he has known the Robinsons for many years. *Ci conosciamo da molti anni.* Peter Robinson adds that they are hoping to purchase a *casa di campagna*. There is a small circular table fixed to the floor in front of my chair and I put my head on it and sleep for a while. It is a cluttered, gray-lighted sleep suffused with the hum of the ferry and with the same feeling of familiarity, which, now that my eyes are closed and it has nothing to fix on, washes over me in unstructured waves until my knowledge of where I am and what I am doing has been broken up and mingled with things I have thought or dreamed or imagined, mingled and mingled into a gray expanse like the sea, with just a few Italian verbs floating on the surface. When I sit up again the northern coast of France is lying in a rocky beige-colored crust along the horizon. A piercing female voice begins to issue from the loudspeaker warning us of the imminent closure of the canteen.

These tidings do not concern us: we are finished with this boat. We strain for release from its numb enchantment. The children are hurling their felt-tip pens back into their rucksacks and urging us into our coats. We go out on deck as the cliffs of Dieppe bear down on us and the wind whirls in a crazed cyclone on the ferry's snub front, lifting our hair into maniac shapes, tugging at our clothes. The melancholy Dieppe sky is deep gray, its sand-colored rocks friable-seeming and transitory. It looks like a place that would forget itself if it could. After a while we go back inside and file along toward the back of the boat, where people are forming long migratory queues and a girl in a white uniform is clearing piles of smeared plates from the tables and the voice on the loud-speaker is bidding us farewell and a safe onward journey.

∝

The road out of Dieppe winds round and round, round and round and round its empty green hinterland, as aimless and methodical as a geriatric waltz around a deserted dance floor. Beneath a sky the color of smelted iron, raw patches of development stand out on the hills above the port: new supermarkets and warehouses, half-built roads, modern buildings standing in empty car parks, a double row of giant streetlights heading inexplicably off into a field. From a distance, the inharmonious spectacle of these cre-ations, in which no one object relates to any other, gives it an ap-pearance of almost human inwardness and alienation, like a crowd of total strangers caught in a random moment on a police security camera. We pass a building like a child's drawing of a Swiss chalet and a building like a cardboard box and a building like a playground climbing frame painted in primary colors. We pass Gemo and Mr. Bricolage and Decathlon. We pass a low, ranchlike building in a tundra of tarmac called Buffalo Grill, with a giant pair of white plastic cow's horns attached to its tiled roof. The air-temperature gauge on the dashboard reads twelve degrees Celsius. The sky looks swollen and bruised. We revolve three times around a roundabout trying to identify the road to Rouen. The roundabout is planted with clumps of marigolds in forensic rows, like a cemetery. I wonder what became of the human instinct for beauty, why it vanished so abruptly and so utterly, why our race should have fallen so totally out of sympathy with the earth. An hour out of Dieppe, a shout goes up from the back seat. We are running through somber green countryside now, past meadows grazed by white Charolais cows, past flat affectless fields under low skies, past narrow little lanes that meander out of sight like unfinished sentences. The children have observed that the temperature gauge has risen by two full degrees. An hour later, on the other side of Rouen, they shout again.

In the front seat we are discussing names. My husband has tired of his name: at forty-one, he wishes to change it. This is an unusual wish, but it does not surprise me. As a small child he was sent to boarding school, where his name was a graven fact on every sock and book and toothbrush in his possession, on the toy rabbit he hugged so hard over the years that it became crushed flat, on the metal trunk he dragged behind him along the platform, beside the waiting train; inscribed on the polished plate trophies won by long-disbanded teams, on watches and pens and handkerchiefs, on yellowed monogrammed towels. He has an antique silver christening mug engraved with his initials—ACC—and there are portraits of his ancestors, frowning clerics, on his parents' walls. It is almost as though his name, so concrete and indelible, preceded him in everything he did so that he was forever dogged by a sense of obligation. I do not know what this is like, only that it is the opposite of what the artist feels when he puts his name to a canvas. It is the opposite of self-expression. As a child my own name seemed strange to me, abstract, like a mathematical symbol whose representative function remained mysterious even once I'd grown accustomed to what it looked like. It was only when I began to write books and put my name to them that I understood its associative purpose. All the same, an artist might prefer a name less constricted by his mortal soul. The artists of the Renaissance often had such names: Veronese ("the man from Verona"), il Tintoretto ("the dyer's son"), il Perugino ("the bloke from Perugia"). A few years ago ACC discarded his profession, removed his name from the company letterhead and the ledger of good works. He began to take photographs, portraits of people whose names he writes out in full. They are unknown people, though at a certain level—police files, prison records, social security databases—their citations are as numerous and indelible as ACC's own. This explains part of his attraction to them. But now he wants a new name to call himself when he looks through the camera lens. I suggest Ace, or even *the* Ace. It seems to me to be just what is required. Go on, I say; why don't you?

We are barreling toward Paris now, which sits on the map like a great glamorous spider in its web. The road has become crowded. There are old, slouching cars with winking indicators and big glittering ogre-like cars with black windows, tiny battered cars with frantic plumes of smoke fluttering from their exhausts and cars towing enormous caravans. There are trucks and lorries and untidy vans of every description, all blaring their horns. The children play Sweet and Sour out of the window. They wave and smile at everyone who passes. The Sweets wave and smile back. The Sours don't. The children keep a tally on a piece of paper. As we near the Paris *périphérique* the road becomes a torrent, an onward rush of roaring, barging traffic all hurtling with carefree ferocity toward the center. In a way I would like to join it: I don't know, perhaps it would be easier. Always the effort of resistance, of countermotion, of breaking off into what is untried and unknown: yet the unknown seems in its distance and blank mystery to contain for me a form of hope, a strange force that is pure possibility. Overhead the sky has come apart in great fraying scarves of pale gray and blue. Bursts of soft sunlight fall and fade and bloom again on the windscreen of the car. The temperature rises another notch. On the back seat, the census of the human disposition finds that people are in general more sweet than sour. Weaving and hesitating and being abused on all sides, we swing gloriously south, onto the Autoroute du Soleil.

FRENCH NIGHTS

Monsieur's garden is well advanced into springtime, though we left home this morning still in the bitter purview of winter. Here the trees are in leaf and there are flowers in the beds. We have been forwarded like clocks by a whole season.

But it is April, and spring, in England too. The sullen English skies seem unkind from the sanctuary of Monsieur's garden, and intentionally cruel; as though the wind and rain that did not modulate by day or night but persisted week after week through February and March, like irreconcilable grief or anger, were the product of temperament rather than latitude. But it is not warmth that I expect from my parent nation: it is beauty, and distinctness. It is delicacy I require and feel cheated of, the delicacy of poets; not warmth, which is for babies. In January, meeting a friend at Bristol airport, I stood at the arrivals gate and watched as people poured in from the Canary Islands, from Tenerife. Back they came, in their shorts and string vests and sombreros, in their tanned orange skin; back they came to the bad-tempered homeland and went whooping out through the automatic doors into its dark and inhospitable evening. In a way I envied them. I have never been able to evade the issue so, with human beings or with anything else. There has to be a reckoning, an accounting. There has, at some point, to be the truth.

Monsieur answers the door himself, apparently alone except for a proud white stiff-haired little dog that might be Tintin's Snowy in his comfortable dotage. Who are we, Monsieur wants to know. He stands in the doorway of his château, diffident in scuffed deck shoes and faded canvas shorts that show his weathered knotty legs from the knee, while Snowy struts with arthritic dignity among the flower beds. Monsieur is in his late fifties or so, slightly wild-haired and abstracted but not unkind-looking. He has little fiercely glittering eyes whose irises are a benevolent sky blue. He advertised his château as offering bed and breakfast, though perhaps he has forgotten it. I tell him we have come to stay the night. *Les Anglais*, I add. *Ah oui*, he says at last, *Les Anglais*! He surveys the two children with an eye that expresses a well-bred tolerance for certain weaknesses. Perhaps when we have unloaded our bags we will be so kind as to put our car in the field. Then he will show us to our rooms. He points to the field, which lies just beyond the avenue of trees through which we came. I wonder whether we constitute an affront to his domain, with the unaestheticism of our arrival. Our car is dusty and litter strewn: we ourselves are stiff and crumpled and white-faced, and though there is no way it can be proved, Monsieur seems to know that we spent the last hour of our journey singing from one end to the other of the repertoire of *The Sound of Music*.

He slips lightly back through his doorway while the car disgorges its unsavory contents on the graveled drive. The children awkwardly probe the near shores of the front lawn, aloofly observed by Snowy. They look backward, almost physically illiterate, as if they have never seen a garden before in their lives. In the car they were reading *The Cat in the Hat*. They read it aloud: it made me laugh. I have always found Dr. Seuss's world to be a place in which adults may satisfy to the full their unacknowledged need for

surreality. When they were small, a friend of mine once drama-
tized *The Lorax* for them in its entirety, and as she came to the
felling and extinction of the trufula trees, dignified tears rolled
steadily down her cheeks. They watched her reverently; for them,
too, books are the highest reality. They were different in those far-
off days: more distinct and compact, entire unto themselves. They
had not yet gone to school. They burned with autonomous life,
with a force that had not yet been catalogued and named, like
Thing One and Thing Two in *The Cat in the Hat*. Now they are
more like the children in the story, neat and combed, anxious because their mother is out. The Cat is the mother's antithesis, anar-
chic and free, available, unscheduled. And though they might
forget it, those storybook children were bored before the Cat in the
Hat came; bored to tears with that life of order and responsibility,
in which nothing ever happened, until one day it did.

When we have our bags and the car is in its field, we present
ourselves again at the front door in a straggling group. Monsieur
immediately manifests himself from an inner chamber. In his
hand are two large old-fashioned iron keys. He leads us into a pale
paneled hallway with glass doors to either side, through which I
can see long perspectives of light-filled rooms like galleries, with
floors so varnished that they shimmer like the surface not of wood
but of water; rooms full of paintings and mirrors, a grand piano,
sculptures and oriental rugs, great fronded plants in china pots,
chairs and tables with elaborately scrolled legs, a vast pale marble
fireplace and great numbers of tall windows with folded shutters,
on the other side of which stands the garden again, so that the
whole place has an appearance of transparency, as if it were made
of glass.

Monsieur noiselessly ascends a broad stone staircase that rises
through the center of the house and we follow, turning through re-

gions of mysterious, untenanted elegance, past glimpses of arched
doorways and distant, glimmering windows, of vanishing hallways
and furniture in a sleep of antiquity, up and up until we come to
the top, where the windows look out at the fat golden hills of Bur-
gundy and Monsieur finally engages his key. We stand behind him
on the painted floorboards of a large landing in the eaves. Under
the window an ancient rocking horse with a coarse, mellifluous
mane and tail and fiery black nostrils waits on its curved runners,
as though for some remembered childhood rider to come again.
There is a little toy carriage too, rickety and antique, and a doll
with pale ringlets and staring china eyes in a tiny chair. Monsieur
opens a door and shows us into a low, large room with red walls. It
is the nursery, he explains: the toys outside once belonged to the
children of the house. I had not suspected Monsieur of sentimentality, and indeed it is sentimentality of a rigid and proprietous
kind, for the same force that requires the children to sleep in the
nursery dictates that their parents should spend the night in a room
far away, a grand room on a lower floor with window seats and a
balcony and a view of the park, where they might never be found.
I wonder what became of the aforementioned children of the
house, and their mother, for Monsieur seems unflinchingly alone.
The color of the nursery, cozy as it is, brings to mind the Red
Room in *Jane Eyre*, in all its punitive reputation. But Monsieur is
not to be offended: we put our bags in the appropriate places and
regroup on the stone staircase, where with the tolerant look again
in his eye, as if he knows of our mildly regrettable English weak-
ness for breakfast, he informs us of the hour at which he serves it.

Outside, the trees in the park cast sharp-edged shadows; the
pale-colored château stands in its own deepening aura of obscurity, seeming to grow paler as evening advances, as though it might

finally dissolve. The air is warm and still: only the pallor of the sky and the sharpness of the shadows betray the fact that it is not yet summer here, in these benignant rolling fields with their foliage already lush. We are south of Paris, north of Dijon, and a few miles west of Auxerre and the river Yonne, whose landscapes Françoise Sagan describes as representing the eternal boredom and beauty of the French *paysage*. This is the heartland of fine wine and fine food: satisfaction and plenty seem to roll off its plump yellow hills. Nearby lies the village of Noyers, in whose soft golden buildings the fat, rich, productive spirit of the soil makes itself fully manifest. In a little bar on the main square we play *babyfoot* and drink wine from tulip-shaped glasses while boys on bicycles and scooters whir up and down the pavements outside. The bar is full of men, who look at us with brazen, friendly curiosity, and indeed there must be something extruded and untranslatable about us, beset as we are by the joy of escape and by the knowledge that we who consumed porridge in a Sussex village that morning have found our way, by a mixture of randomness and design, here.

There are one or two restaurants nearby. They have an appearance of Masonic discretion. We peer into their dimly lit interiors from the pavement. We scan their uncompromising menus. We have been awake a long time. Is it possible that this same day will oblige us to scale the treacherous peaks of *haute cuisine*, with the children roped to our backs? We recall that Monsieur suggested the pizzeria: at the time this seemed a form of veiled insult, but his economy of manner proved again deceptive. The pizzeria is perfectly correct: Monsieur could have told us it would be so. This is not the moment to induct minors in *spécialités du terroir*, no, no! They must eat simple food and be hurried back to the nursery *tout de suite*! And indeed they take to their beds in the Red Room with unwonted gratitude and remain there all night, under the bridled eye of the rocking horse and the wide-awake gaze of the china doll.

In the morning I walk across the fields in a bright, arid light. When I return I can hear the grand piano being played through the open windows. I stand in the garden and listen. The lucidity of the sound seems more real to me than anything we have left behind us, than home, than the days whose repetition had laid a kind of fetter on my soul. In its solitariness it speaks to my own single nature. It startles me a little, to be spoken to; as though I have been silent, absent, unconscious; as though my life, the life of home, were a fake, and the real life was roaming somewhere in the world, fleet-footed, unique, uncapturable, to be glimpsed sometimes through an open window, and then to vanish again.

 C∼

By afternoon we are down in the Rhône valley, west of the Rhône Alps, east of the Ardèche. Lyons lies behind us, and the Saône. The temperature gauge is singing like a canary; the clear light of the Mediterranean is filling the dry green basins of Montélimar. It is five o'clock. We are searching for the establishment where we are to spend the night, the house of a man named Bertrand. Bertrand's domain is at once more *outré*, more esoteric, and more aesthetically confounding than Monsieur's. It takes a long time to find it; and when we do it is as thick in its own enchanted slumber as Sleeping Beauty's castle.

There are strange pelted hills that rise like a dromedary's humps from the plain. We wind around them, asking directions of everyone we see. The hills are fragrant, forested with brittle chestnut trees and herbs and carpeted with twigs and dried leaves that crackle underfoot. At the very end of a narrow road that twirls abstractedly upward through the wilderness and is then extinguished, we find a potholed track traversing the hillside. At the end of that is a very high stone wall with a pair of giant doors in it that are resolutely closed. There is no doorbell or knocker; there isn't another house for miles around either. But our directions were increasingly clear; there can be no mistake: we are certain Bertrand is in there somewhere.

Presently we try one of the doors and its great iron handle turns, admitting us into a large stone courtyard. The courtyard is completely enclosed: the wildly forested hillside grows up all around its perimeter. Yet inside it is spacious, orderly, well tended. There are no weeds in the borders: the flowers spill from their stone urns by intention, not neglect. They have recently been watered: bright beads still tremble on their petals. Yet everything is silent: there is no one here. In fairy tales, such places are the deepest emanations of magic: the castle in its forest of thorns, the mountain room unlocked by a keyhole in the ice, the lake with its pleasure boats that lies beneath the floorboards. It is in the elision of the human hand that the magic expresses itself. A fire burns with no one to stoke it; a meal stands hot on the table in an empty house. Here, there is a room, not inside but out: it stands in the right angle of the courtyard, two sides of which, I now see, are formed by an old house. It has a large low roof supported by a pillar on its far corner. Under it there are beautiful rugs, and an arrangement of furniture. There are two long sofas, an armchair, a baroque standard lamp, a mahogany coffee table, a bookshelf, and a parrot in a cage hanging from the rafters. We cross to the front door and ring the bell, which unexpectedly makes the noise of a croaking frog. Then we sit down on the sofas: they are extremely comfortable. Ten minutes pass, perhaps more. At last the door quietly opens and a man slips out of the shadows of the

house and into the sun. This is Bertrand. A squat little dog with a
bunched-up face like a boxer's fist slowly follows him. Bertrand
greets us with quiet sincerity. He is sorry he took so long to come:
he was asleep.

Like Monsieur, Bertrand is in his late fifties, or perhaps a little
older; and like Monsieur he appears to operate alone. He wears
the same outfit of canvas shorts and scuffed deck shoes. But he has
something delicate and hopeful about him, something of the
choirboy or cherub; something childlike, with his full curving
mouth and large tremulous eyes and soft fine white curling hair,
with his inconvenient afternoon nap. An enormous white cat has
followed the little dog out into the courtyard. These are Pollux and
Nestor. Bertrand excuses himself: he must make a small adjustment to our rooms. One of the beds he has made up for the children will be, he now sees, too small. He must *aménager*. We will do
him the kindness of waiting.

My tutored female soul is alerted by the prospect of Bertrand,
white-haired and eminent as he seems, *aménaging* alone. I am even
a little outraged on his behalf. What English male of nearly pen-
sionable age bestirs himself to ensure that children are in beds of
the proper sizes, even for a modest fee? Bertrand reappears and we
are ushered inside. The house is as puzzle-like and perplexing inside as out. Its rooms all face different ways and seem to live in distinct eras. There is a kitchen out of a Victorian novel, with copper
molds and saucepans on the walls and an iron range in front of
which I expect to see Mrs. Beeton in a white apron and cap. There
is a large, light, high-ceilinged room full of paintings and modern
furniture like a Parisian atelier. There is a library like a cabinet,
with a door concealed behind the shelves.

Upstairs, at the end of a long, creaking passage, there is a
semicircular window that sheds a strange, spectral light. Our

rooms are ghostly too: they have an air of occupation, with their antique beds and embroidered counterpanes, their oval mirrors and threadbare tapestry rugs. I stand at the window and see the dark, forested hill plunging downward and the countryside far below that reaches on and on into its mounded, mysterious distances. It all seems familiar, though it is not: I feel that I have stood at this window a thousand times and looked out, as I am doing now. This was something I often felt as a child, when I would remember things I had read in books as though I had lived them myself. It never struck me that there was anything wrong with it, though it was disturbing. But sometimes I would read the book again to find what I had remembered so clearly, and discover that it was no longer there.

Later, Bertrand invites us onto the terrace. The terrace has the same view as our bedroom upstairs: it is a view, Bertrand says, of the Ardèche, with its forests and gorges and *massif*. He goes back into the house and returns with an *apéritif*, an unlabeled bottle of effervescent rose-colored wine. A friend of his, a friend who lives on the other side, toward the Rhône Alps, produces it. He thinks we will find that it is very good. Bertrand tells us that he is a native of Paris: until five years ago, he was a city banker. He retired early and bought this house. It was his dream to do so, *aménagement* included, for he needs to be active; besides, it seems natural to him to *faire un succès* with his time. He retains his Paris apartment: the friend with whom he shares this house is there now. Personally he does not like to go to Paris anymore. He would rather be here. He gazes at his view with his melancholic childlike eyes. He has changed for dinner: he is wearing an immaculate white shirt and loafers and a navy cashmere sweater knotted round his shoulders. His fine white waving hair is combed back from his well-modeled face. He is tall and slender in his elderly cherubic beauty. The feeling of enchantment that pervades this house emanates, I now see, from Bertrand himself. He is like a maiden in a fairy tale, all modesty and correctness and virtuous industry, waiting forlornly in his tower.

The children are in the garden with Nestor the dog. The blue pall of evening deepens around them in the trees. Finally, Bertrand suggests that we go in: it is getting dark. He is expecting more people but they have not yet arrived. It is irritating, for dinner must be at eight. He has informed these people of this fact: it is a shame they cannot be punctual. But some people are like that. There is no accounting for them. Distressed as he is, I venture to ask what he wishes me to do with the children. His large, orblike eyes grow larger still. There can be no question: we will all eat together. The food is quite simple. It is merely a question of waiting for the reprobates to arrive. Shortly afterward they do. They are a gray, narrow, pinched-looking couple: they have been walking all day in the Ardèche and misjudged the time it would take them to get back. It is a little inconvenient, *ce loisir*, is it not? And the road is so potholed, so slow! The woman's pale, angular cheeks wear a hectic pink flush beneath her spectacles. The man is bearded and severe. Bertrand brings more glasses. We arrange ourselves in the cultured sitting room, with its canvases and totemic masks and abstract sculptural forms. Beyond the large windows the vast, watery, blue-tinged darkness deepens. The other couple reveal that they have been staying at Bertrand's for the whole week. Tomorrow they return to Lyons. It is their hobby, to take walking holidays. They take several a year. They have walked in every significant part of France, though not, until now, the Ardèche. They have not been disappointed by the Ardèche, though it does not attain the heights of their favorite, the Cévennes. The Cévennes are nearby, as are the Rhône Alps, another favorite of theirs. But this area certainly has its merits.

Bertrand announces that dinner is ready. We pass through the house, through the circular hall, through a passageway that elides the kitchen and twists and turns, and into a long vaulted stone room with great glass doors all along one side. This, I now see, forms the end of the courtyard that is at right angles to the house. The table is shrouded in white damask, laden with candelabra, silverware, and glass. We are served hot asparagus and tissue-thin leaves of smoked ham. We are served pale yellow wine from a crystal decanter, and warm rolls with cold butter. The bearded man and his wife seem to take all this as a matter of course, but we feel an amazement that borders on consternation. What does it signify, all this refinement, this correct and devotional passion for sensual things? At home, certainly, I often felt that our life lacked beauty: I looked for it in music, in poetry and painting, sometimes in the world itself, when a particular evening sky or fall of light, a glimpse of city trees in leaf or of the forms of my children, seemed to become more than itself, to become representational. I would put peonies in a vase, wash the floors, tidy up; but I never found much art in daily things. There was always too much reality, churning just ahead, mixing everything together into a gray, agitated mass. It was only in writing that I could separate them again, and distinguish the bad from the good. But this man Bertrand lives behind a high wall, far from other people. He has asked that only beautiful things come near him. Is this the right way to be? Is it permitted, to turn your back on churning reality?

We ask the bearded man what he does for a living, and he replies that he is retired. We are surprised: he can barely be more than fifty. What was his trade? He says he was an employee of the

French national railway. One retires early there, at fifty, and the pension, a final-salary scheme, is very generous. The bearded man is rather defensive as he relays these facts. Bertrand explains that there are many French people who find the arrangement somewhat unfair, outrageous even, and the bearded man sits erect while the explanation is given. Then he proceeds to cut up his food and place the pieces methodically in his mouth. Bertrand watches him, a glint in his eye. This couple have irritated him, gray and complacent and ungiving as they are. They swallow his food without comment; they weigh up his domain coldly, rationally, indifferent to all but their own preferences. Why does he expose himself to the world in this way? I don't believe he does it entirely for money: there is no need to treat us as lavishly as he does. He does it, perhaps, for the same reason that artists show their work, for the same reason I choose to publish the books I write rather than lock them in a drawer. Indeed, this couple have their exact equivalent in the field of literary criticism. It doesn't trouble them at all that they could never create something beautiful, as Bertrand has. Nonetheless, their presence here indicates that after all Bertrand does need the world, so that it may look on what he has done. In the end he needs reality, to measure his creation against.

But Bertrand wants to talk about *les Anglais*. He has the impression that the English male, in his most fully realized form—the English politician, for example—is more various, more cultivated, more *branché* somehow than his French equivalent. He has a broader knowledge of life, a bigger range. He heard such a man talking on the radio the other day, a politician, what was his name? Douglas Hurd. This Douglas Hurd was a man of culture and sensitivity and yet also a man of power. In France this is unthinkable. The man of culture is a man of culture, the politician a politician. Bertrand has by now served us with a melting *feuilleté de poissons*, a salad of crisp herbs and leaves and lemon, and a new, paler wine from another crystal decanter. I say that probably the English male is troubled by precisely the same feelings about the French. I am not entirely certain that this is true. Bertrand nods his large head thoughtfully and disappears into the kitchen. The two children have eaten very little of their food. They were struck dumb by the arrival of the asparagus, and have remained that way for the rest of the evening. They do not dislike asparagus: on the contrary, at home they eat it often. But they appear surprised to have met it here, amid the spectacle of Bertrand's dining room. The wife of the bearded man is looking at them with the diffident French expression that I always mistake for disapproval—though this time it turns out that I am right. I ask her whether a French child would have eaten everything on its plate. Of course, she says. She does not care for my veiled English compliment: she merely shrugs at my obtuseness. A French child eats what it is given. It has to be done from the beginning, she adds, lest I am thinking of making up for lost time by forcing the food down their throats then and there.

There is a beef stew and more wine, and the conversation goes faster and faster until I cannot keep up. Bertrand sends the dish around for second helpings, and when it is her turn Madame takes the serving spoon and dabs it on her plate, an act that seems hieratic in its significance, like the motions of a priest at the altar. It spots her plate with a portion the size of a fingernail, which she does not touch. Later Bertrand brings chocolate mousse in chilled glasses, decorated with beautiful candied orange peels that wear little half-casings of chocolate. He admits that he made them himself. Afterward I take the children upstairs along the creaking passage. I lie on their bed and read to them, among the dark forms of unfamiliar furniture, while the owls hoot outside. I think of how fortunate it is that there is a word—holiday—which not only explains the experience of going to bed in strange rooms but decrees it to be pleasurable. When I return downstairs it is to find the cognac out and the laughter loud and even Madame grown a little garrulous in her cardigan and blouse and gathered skirt. There is coffee; I ask if I may smoke. Of course, says Bertrand solemnly, I myself was once a great smoker. *J'étais un grand fumeur.* It sounds like the beginning of a story, but of course it is only the end of one. At some point Bertrand smoked his last cigarette: it is very clear to me, this moment of renunciation. It decorates him like a priestly robe, or a medal. Bertrand has thrown off the temptation to live life without recognizing the finality of all things.

In the morning he is nowhere to be seen. Breakfast is laid out on a round table in the hall, the coffee mysteriously hot and the croissants warm from the oven, like Beauty's supper in the Beast's castle. There are esoteric jams, homemade, in white china bowls: they are chestnut and walnut and fig from the dry, scented hillside. Later Bertrand appears and shows us his library with its extraordinary collection of antique volumes, which his mother bequeathed him after her death. He was very close to his mother: now she has become these books that stand in her son's room, with their densely typed pages and faded beautiful spines; these motionless creatures that rest finished on their shelves while day and night come and go at the window, beating like soft waves against their buried knowledge.

∾

Colors fade: we pass through warm, silent landscapes whose ocher and rust-red and flat, ancient green seem so old and primitive that it is surprising to see houses on the hills or sunk in the distances of the plains. The wind turbines look like strange gods, with their triad heads turning under the blue sky. Later we wind through a spectral, blackened landscape where forest fires have left charred skeletons of trees: it is like a grove of death, the hills coming down steeply to the road and the road winding and turning among them so that nothing but their desolate slopes and petrified forms can be seen. Then all at once we are out, with the mineral-blue Mediterranean sparkling below us and the white Palladian vista of settlements frilled with surf, of Cannes and Antibes and St. Raphaël, stretching all along the hazy shoreline of the Côte d'Azur. We have traveled from one sea to another, from one world to another: suddenly there are palm trees on the roadside and warm maritime breezes and a feeling of liberty, of an almost physical unburdening, like a winter coat being taken off, a pair of heavy shoes unlaced and hurled into the glittering water. All of us feel it, this change: we whoop and cheer as we soar down toward the Baie des Anges. We have closed the door on England as one would close the door on a dark and cluttered house and walk out into the sun. It is this release, from the feeling of interiority, that I relish the most. Yet I love its darkness and clutter, its shady labyrinths of memory and emotion. They give rise to feelings of outward misshapenness, but they have their own value, the heavy metal coins of Englishness that strain and bulge through the fabric of the purse. But now the purse is empty: it is flat and light. We roll down the windows and everything begins to flutter madly, our hair and clothes, our books and bags and sweet wrappers, a whole deck of cards that whirls around like a crazy summer snowstorm, while outside the light leaps and dances on the water and the little boats pirouette in the bay, and a plane like a child's toy turns in the sky to make its landing at the toy airport of Nice.

In the late afternoon we arrive at Cap Ferrat. We are staying here, on the threshold of Italy: tomorrow we will cross over. The

promontory is so still and miniature that it might be made out of
plaster. The pastel light grows pinker as the sun declines: the surface of the water is as pale as milk. Behind the walls of 1920s man-
sions, perfumed gardens begin to emit the pulse of evening. The
sea lies quietly in its little pink bays. There is an atmosphere of un-
reality in the motionless air, a sense of the painted backdrop. This
is the habitat of famous actors, of mythmakers: the hand of nature has been stayed. I remember a story a friend told me, of her
small son running barefoot across a stretch of lawn here, his upturned soles dyed green from the grass. And indeed the gardens,
with their topiary and their waxlike flowers, their barbered palm
trees and orderly, rigid, dark green lawns, seem curiously man-
made; more so than the romantic houses, which resemble the
palaces and castles that clouds sometimes make in the sky on a
summer afternoon. A little well-paved path runs all around the
perimeter, just above the sea: people are jogging there, in sunglasses and immaculate white shoes, disappearing around the end
where the sea splashes against the rocks in an orderly fashion, like
a small-scale representation of itself on a stage set.

Our hotel room has a blue-tiled floor and no blankets on the
beds. It is clear that winter does not exist here, merely something
that I imagine to be like a brief coma, an interlude of unknowing
when the houses close their shutters and the gardens stop growing,
when the pink light is switched off and the sea is drained like a
swimming pool out of season. But now it is awakening: there are
people in the cafés; one or two houses have opened their eyes. We
change into different clothes, summer clothes that make us look
white-skinned and startled in the mirror. We do not yet look as we
feel, or feel as we look. We are in some perilous state of preexis-
tence; like unchristened babies, we are not yet saved. The baptism
must commence; there is no time to lose: we run down, down to

the milk-white waters and the pinkish bay, past the deserted hotel terrace with its empty tables, past the mysterious shuttered houses, the pulsing gardens, down to the little crescent of coarse sand, the waiting waters.

One after another we plunge in and swim out, sending long folds across the silken surface. We cry out; we bellow, and send sprays of water into the air like whales. The sea is cold; a wedge of wintry shadow stands across the beach. At the far end a rhombus of sun remains. There are some wooden-slatted loungers there and I see a stirring of bodies amid them. People are sitting up, apparently to observe our maiden voyage into the unseasonal waters of the Mediterranean. They seem astonished, almost affronted; they shade their eyes with brown wrinkled hands glittering with rings, for most of them are elderly ladies, as thin as lizards, with creased skins the color of tobacco. They stir their dark brown limbs and adjust their bikinis and suck the last of the sun from the sky. Occasionally they raise a skinny arm to shade their eyes and look. They are strange, stirring like lizards in their crevice of sun. But to them we are stranger still, with our white skins, our worship of a cold and contradictory element, our dysfunctional joy.

We will not always, I think, be so out of place. We will blend in; eventually we will gain some foliage, some camouflage. But not tonight, crossing and recrossing from shadow into light as evening advances over the motionless waters. Tonight we are migratory creatures, washed in by a powerful current, traversing the bay and pondering the intricate mystery of land.

ITALIAN IN THREE MONTHS

I have taken up with a new textbook: *Italian in Three Months*. This one is a little more personal in its drive toward socialization, though no less prescriptive. *Forgive me, but I'm too tired to play tennis just now.* And indeed, there is no time for tennis, nor any other trivial pursuit: the three months are flying on wings of fire, passing over great continents of vocabulary, mountain ranges of irregular verbs, oceans of tenses and subjunctives where indirect object pronouns swim, sharp-toothed and voracious, awaiting a victim. We are expected to have gained a knowledge of these landmarks merely by gazing at them from a great height. Almost as soon as they come they are gone, into the linguistic past, a place of fundamental risk and confusion where things become unlearned and ungrasped, where pitiful reserves of knowledge are swept away like a pensioner's savings in a financial crash. Unlike the historic past, the linguistic past is subject to incessant change: whole landmasses sink overnight, settlements are razed to the ground, insecure structures are swept away. It matters not that yesterday I knew the central modal verbs and demonstrative adjectives: today they are nowhere to be found. I begin to see that the principle of acceleration is the solitary scientific tenet to be found in *Italian in Three Months*. They have merely removed from language-learning the impediment of time. I might as well be reading *Living in Three Months*, and get the whole thing over and done with.

It is in the area of vocabulary that I feel my resources can be most securely invested. An identifiable object has a kind of neutrality, like Switzerland: it is a place that seems to offer the possibility of agreement. I have no difficulty with an armchair being *una poltrona* or a rug *il tappeto*; indeed, I almost prefer calling a mirror *uno specchio*, for it seems to suit it better. These things, so fixed, make a little circuit of language, as simple as a child's toy. They go and come back punctually along their single track; not heading off into wilderness, among mist-shrouded peaks where meaning mislays itself. I can collect them, solid nouns with a face value, like fat gold coins; I can store them up and exchange them for goods. I ask for *formaggio* and I get it; I request *burro, zucchero, mele*, and they fall into my lap. But sometimes I cannot escape the feeling that the coin in my hand is counterfeit money, for there are other words that have no ring of truth about them at all. They are false somehow; I can't believe they'll work. How could a *scarpa*, for instance, be the same thing as a shoe? If I went into a shop and asked for a pair of *scarpe*, I would surely be handed a brace of woodland fowl, or two fish with particularly bony spines. I am unwilling, moreover, to relinquish the serviceable properties, the reliable-shoe-ness, of my native word. What will become of these qualities when they pass through the dark tunnel of translation? They will be lost, as so much else is lost between languages: nuances and puns and rhymes, all gone astray in the general disorder, like the bags and umbrellas and knitted scarves that accumulate in the Lost Property office at Clapham Junction. I feel a new respect for that go-between, the translator: this, I now see, is a person opposed to waste, to chaos, to the easy-come, easy-go disposability of the modern world. Patiently the translator reunites those bags and umbrellas with their owners, or finds some other use for them, for just as language can lose its raiment so it can accept some borrowed finery. There is a way, I don't doubt, of doing justice to the shoe; the *scarpa* itself probably has some special qualities, though I can't yet imagine them. The Spanish for shoe is *zapato*, which I think of as a very pointed kind of dancing shoe, while the French *chaussure* is a somber gentleman's slipper made of brown leather. The *scarpa* is as yet indistinct. I suspect it has very high sharp heels, and is the sort of thing that might be used as the murder weapon in an Agatha Christie novel.

Italian in Three Months has the usual cast of characters, with the addition of a number of traveling businessmen who are generally to be found propping up the hotel bar in Bologna or Rome, engaging passing females in witless conversation. These men are mostly Americans: they urge alcohol on their gentle companions and loudly insist on paying. Occasionally they are glimpsed at large, on the streets, defending their rights as citizens and refusing to be hoodwinked by dishonest Italian shopkeepers. *No, it is your fault. You gave me the wrong change. Please call the owner.* The Italians, meanwhile, pass the time in melodious flights of cultural self-satisfaction, purchasing buffalo mozzarella from the delicatessen, ordering *gnocchi* at Mamma Rosa's restaurant, taking their coffee *espresso*, with a shot of spirits if they're in the mood. They are brisk but not impolite toward Hugh O'Sullivan, who wants to buy a *casa di campagna*, and remain quite calm with Jeff and Bill, who present themselves almost daily at the doctor's surgery in a condition of mild hysteria. Peter, a solitary Englishman, is glimpsed every now and then hopelessly trying to make his way to an assignation with an Italian woman called Luisa. He wanders the streets asking directions; later he is seen at a bus stop, importuning passersby: when he finally locates Luisa as agreed on the Piazza Navona, he blurts out that he has just witnessed an acquaintance being run over by a scooter. I sense the hand of E. M. Forster somewhere deep in Peter's past: this is the type of Englishman whom the Luisas of this world will forever try to understand but fail, whom they will follow diligently around the hospitals of Rome, searching for his injured "friend," whom he seems to care for so profoundly.

I learn the word for boring, which is *noioso*, and for fear, which is *paura*. I learn the words for hunger, truth, kindness, passion, tragedy, success. I learn to say, *I am in a hurry*. I learn to say, *I am a shop assistant*.

∞

The Garfagnana is cloaked in cloud; the melancholy hills of Barga make giant shapes that vanish upward into mist. There is a whole community of Scots that originated here: within the steep, narrow streets of the town a Scottish museum occupies two floors of a *palazzo* with pitted pale plaster like a bad complexion. Apparently, a delegation from Prestwick makes its way to Barga every year. The new direct flight from Prestwick to nearby Pisa has been a cause for celebration, in this place where tiny three-wheeled Piaggios buzz like hornets along the ancient alleyways and people hang their washing out of high windows; where the cathedral stands on its lonely hilltop, a vision of travertine austerity, and gazes out of its weathered face at the Apennines.

We came here over the white Apuan mountains, leaving behind the rose-colored light of the coast, the belle époque charm of Santa Margherita and Portofino; up and up into regions of dazzling ferocity where we wound among deathly white peaks scarred with marble quarries, along glittering chasms where the road fell away into nothingness and we clung to our seats in terror. The Italians, we have learned, are supreme artists in what I had thought to

be a humdrum science, that of road building. When we crossed
the border at Ventimiglia we were immediately initiated into these
arts: there was, it seemed, to be no more tedious snaking around,
no timid twisting and turning, no quarter given to the lush moun-
tainous terrain that tumbled down toward the sea. The Italians do
not drive around a mountain, no, no: they go straight through it.
We must have driven through forty or fifty of them in our first two
hours in the country. We have become blasé: that is why the road

to Garfagnana is so unnerving. Clearly we have done something incorrect by coming up here, something an Italian would never do, unless he was driving one of the giant dusty lorries heaped with rough chunks of rock that we encounter at hairpin bends on their way from the quarries down to the coast. Each time we find one there, we scream like people in a horror film. The road ravels on and on, through vertiginous passes like the eye of a needle, through desert-like valleys, creeping along a shelf high over a vast drop where a moonscape of peaks extends to the horizon, the white marble glinting like death in its fastnesses of rock. Consulting the map, we see that there was a businesslike road from the coast that skirted the mountains and would have delivered us in an hour or so to our destination. We ought to have taken it; and yet it seems strange, the thought that we might have remained ignorant of this cold and savage place, might never have known the real truth, in our somnambulant treading of well-worn paths. Instead we are having a thorough and passionate encounter with fear. During the nights that follow, I wake up several times dreaming that I am still on that road, for I am certain that one day I will see its like again. Amid its voids and vacuums I discern a detailed image of my own mortality.

We are staying for a few days in a little house on the side of a hill, where at night it rains and rains and the clouds hang all day in the valley. It is a *casa di campagna* of a rather hemmed-in variety: there is a chicken farm next door, and houses where dogs bark incessantly at the wire fences, and down in the damp of the valley floor we find an English couple who came here on holiday and never left. They were in their early twenties at the time: now they must be more than forty. They too have dogs, big ones with wolfish pelts and pricked-up ears who gallop far ahead of them as they walk up the hill past our house. Once or twice I look up and there they are, two giant animals that have landed in the shaggy garden with a great bound to announce the imminent arrival of their masters. They have mournful faces, this couple, and are constantly to be seen in elaborate wet-weather gear, which contributes to their air of pessimism. They roam the fields and lanes like unquiet souls whom a twenty-year curse has locked out of their native land.

It is strange to be in a house again, to cook our own food, to make a fire in the little terracotta woodburner which emits great puffs of smoke when the wind blows the wrong way down the chimney. The children play on a long roped swing in the garden. They sit one on top of the other and go back and forth, back and forth like a pendulum. Sometimes we go to the local town, whose fortifications and *loggia* and graceful squares are all exactly as they should be. The children say *buongiorno* and *grazie*. We buy pecorino and prosciutto and olives from the delicatessen. We buy pasta in the shape of scrolls and butterflies and shells. The man in the delicatessen conforms startlingly to the character of Luigi the shopkeeper in *Italian in Three Months*. He says *Desidera?* and *Basta così?* He hands us our purchases in paper bags. Then we return to the little house, where great ragged gray clouds drift slowly along the valley and accumulate around the hills.

It is not, somehow, as we expected it to be. It is as if we have entered a cul-de-sac at great speed. Things have ground abruptly, a little jarringly, to a halt. Time has started to back up around us: there is a sense of things thickening, congealing, of familiar atmospheres re-forming. After the exhilaration of escape, we find that we are all still here, unaltered. But we did not come here to find ourselves: we came for something we are able to identify only by its absence. We grow bad-tempered. When we go to the local town the children shove each other and cry, or run away from us, laughing shrilly. They no longer say *buongiorno*: they are not one-trick ponies. We have lost the thread a little. Did we come all the way here to behave exactly as we do at home, while dogs bark at the wire fences and the mist hangs sodden on the hills, and the chickens in the chicken farm scream inside their metal sheds? What exactly are we meant to *do*? The English couple pass by in the rain and talk about the renovations to their house, which are still in progress twenty years on.

We have arranged to stay a whole week in the *casa di campagna*. We go for walks; we go to Barga, though I draw a line at the Scottish museum. On the fourth day we decide to go to Lucca. Lucca is an hour away by train, but it is apparent that no one is enjoying the sensation of the Garfagnanan grass growing under their feet. Above the train station the sky is a pale gray blank; the station is deserted. After a while there are a few people on the platform. They sit and read newspapers or talk on their mobile phones. They seem a little more connected to the world, a little more current, than Luigi the shopkeeper or our English neighbors. My spirits begin to revive. A smart, slender woman is standing nearby, talking into her phone. First she has a long conversation in Italian. Then she has a long conversation in English. She is American, though she has the groomed look of a native. Her conversation concerns her studies in art history, her frenetic social calendar, her retinue of Italian friends whose demands on her she is hard put to satisfy. She mentions her apartment in Lucca: she is on her way there now. I listen to her admiringly; I look at her immaculate clothes, her delicate *scarpe*, her polished fingernails tapping on the casing of her telephone. I am glad that she has got herself so beautifully organized, for sometimes it seems to me that human beings are only chaotic and blind, are all fettered unconsciousness, strug-

gling in their self-imposed chains as I feel myself in that moment
to be.

We board the train and pass along the Serchio valley, among
gentle green perspectives of hills and distant mountains, past
melancholy Barga, swaying serenely over grassy plains and stop-
ping sometimes at deserted stations that seem to stand in the middle of nowhere. There are weeds flowering on their platforms, and
clumps of grass between the rails, and after a while we slowly pull
away again. I feel that something new is disclosing itself, something to do with time. We are free: no one is expecting us. We look
out of the windows. We listen to the tranquil hum of the engine.
We watch the valley in the mild morning light.

∞

Lucca stands in an unbroken circle of gigantic walls. They are
forty or fifty feet high, dark, and so thick that over time they have
become a land formation, a strange circular isthmus with lawns
and trees and paths on the top. They were built in the sixteenth
century to keep out the Tuscans, those gentle Chianti-quaffing folk,
and now, in their retirement, with their neat paths and barbered
lawns, they provide tourists with a circular bicycle ride and a view
of the plains and mountains from their colossal shoulders. Outside
them the city has spread its clutter, its traffic and car parks and res-
idential suburbs, its strings of shops: within, in the old town, an atmosphere of unusual refinement prevails. Every infelicitous speck
of modernity has been sieved out. When those walls were built, it
was in ignorance of what they would be called on over time to re-
pel: Tuscans or car parks, it's all the same to them. Of course,
these beautiful islands of the past in their turbid oceans of modernity are to be found all over Europe, in England too. At the heart

of every hideous human settlement we find an image of our pre-
deceased ancestor, aestheticism. It is our lot to defend that image,
lifeless as it may seem. But the forbidding walls of Lucca do a
more thorough job of it than most.

The bicycle is the accepted means of transportation here: the
motionless air rings with their shrilling bells. Resolute bluestockings fly by with a warning *glissando*; professorial men in tweed jackets glide past, erect, with a *ping!* Groups of students and tourists
pass along the old paved streets in weaving flocks, their many bells
trilling and squawking as they go. For a while we walk, but we are
birds without wings. We return to the city gates, where earlier we
passed numerous bicycle shops without realizing their significance.
There we are given bicycles at a daily rate, in descending sizes like
the furniture of the bear family that so preoccupied Goldilocks,
whose tastes and proportions ruled their little owner to the degree
that she could feel no sympathy with the world. I have never cared
for the moral of that story, nor for Goldilocks either: but the bears

in their shameless conservatism I like least of all. I do not want to
be Mrs. Bear, with her middle-sized possessions, her brown moth-
erliness, her sturdy bear's body that contrasts so with the blond
whimsicality of her intruder. I do not want to be the Bear family,
pedaling sedately on their bicycles of descending sizes.

But it is too late: up we go, up to the ramparts, where a breeze
rustles the great skirts of the trees and the laid-out paths and
lawns, so strangely elevated, recede down their long, curving perspectives. It is four kilometers all the way round: on one side there
is the plain with its dove-gray light, its pale geometry of roads and
buildings and here and there the classical forms of Lucchese villas,
sunk in their soft beds of trees; on the other there is the slowly revolving ancient town. We see its bell towers and palaces, its piazzas and churches, the Guinigi Tower with its mysterious forested
top, all seeming to turn like a jeweled mechanical city pirouetting
on a music box. We go faster and faster, flying along the gravel
paths, whirling through colonnades of trees, but the strange feeling persists that we aren't moving at all; that the city is rotating
while we are standing still.

In the afternoon we wander the paved streets: we visit the Piazza dell'Anfiteatro, which stands on the site of a Roman amphitheater and retains its cruel elliptical shape. It has vaulted sides
with low archways that faintly suggest the introduction of victims,
though there are cafés there now and souvenir shops. The children
buy a souvenir each, a little china bell and a ceramic bowl with
Lucca written on them. There are people here, people in the
churches and the cafés, up the towers and on the streets. They
seem perfectly satisfied with all this magnificence: they seem content. They look at the Roman remains and the Palazzo Pretorio.
They lunch in the Piazza Napoleone, named after Napoleon's sister Elisa, who once governed the principality of Lucca. What is it

to them, I wonder, this place whose layers reach down so strangely, so intricately into time like a crevasse into the frozen mystery of a glacier? What, in a personal sense, does it signify? They come to marvel at the sublimity and passion that human beings once were capable of: I wonder why its monuments fail to shake them out of their composure. Do they not want to be passionate themselves, and sublime? Why do they care so much for it, with their video cameras and guidebooks and long lenses, with their money belts and sensible shoes, when it cares so little for them?

In the Piazza San Martino is the *duomo*. Its tiered tower is slightly askew and its front with its three colonnaded layers has an ornamental severity, like the lace on an old lady's mantilla. It seems a little reproachful, in its gray and delicate austerity. The bluestockings whir by, ringing their bells. There is a sculpture above the porch, of a man with a cloak and a sword on horseback. Another man stands beside him: the cloaked rider is turned toward him, though not to smite him down. It is his own cloak his sword is directed at, for he is St. Martin, who was asked for alms on a cold day by a wayside beggar and unexpectedly responded by sawing his garment into two. The beggar was presumably pleased: half a cloak, I suppose, is better than no cloak at all. The night after this event, St. Martin is said to have seen a vision of Jesus in a dream, wearing the half he gave away. I am surprised by this: visions of Jesus rarely advocate the morality of fifty percent. Inside the *duomo* we see the sculpture of St. Martin again. The one outside is a copy: the original has been brought in, to protect it from the weather. It is more affecting, this ancient, eroded image, for its symbolism has become the unique form of its vulnerability. The rain and the wind have rubbed away at St. Martin: he may as well not have kept his fifty percent after all. He shields but he is unshielded, and were it not for the different kindness of our curatorial age he would be whittled down to a peg of stone.

Nearby there is a painting by Tintoretto of the Last Supper. It is small, or perhaps it is merely crowded, for it contains many figures. Generally Tintoretto's human beings are large things: life is all, or seems to be. And indeed the figure of Jesus at the far end of the table is the painting's furthest and smallest point, as though to express the remoteness of the conceptual, of self-sacrifice, in a busy room where a woman reclines breast-feeding her baby in the foreground and men are leaning across the table to talk, eager living men with brown skin and muscular arms, talking and gesticulating around a table laden with food and wine. The two men at the nearest end of the table are distinctively dressed: one wears a purple tailored coat, and the other has the sleeves of his shirt rolled up to the biceps. They are talking together: they possess a great reality, the reality of the living moment, of the chunks of bread and the half-drunk glasses of wine, of the plates and crumpled tablecloth and the woman who watches their conversation instead of the baby at her breast.

I look at this painting for a long time. I try to understand it. I try to understand the difference between the people close to Jesus at the far end of the table and the people down at this end, close to us. The closer they are to us, the less attention they pay him. Yet it is more beautiful down here; it is richer and more alive. At the other end, Jesus bends to put bread in the bearded mouth of Peter and Peter ardently clasps his hands. That, too, is a moment of life in this painted scene. I don't doubt that Tintoretto believed it himself. But the reality of the man in the purple coat, whose hand rests on a fallen keg of wine, is too powerful. Perception is stronger than belief, at least for an artist, who sees such grandeur in ordinary

The Last Supper, c. 1592, by Tintoretto (1518–94)

things. In this it is the artist who is God. And it is a strange kind of proof we seek from him, we who are so troubled by our own mortality, who know we will all eat a last supper of our own. We want the measure of the grandeur taken. We want to know that life was indeed what it seemed to be.

On the train home we find our guidebook in a bag, and discover that we have seen virtually nothing of the glories of Lucca, neither the National Museum nor the Villa Guinigi, neither the Filippino Lippi altarpieces nor the della Quercia engravings. The children sit in a corner, studying their souvenirs. Later we will learn to fillet an Italian city of its artworks with the ruthless efficiency of an English aristocrat deboning a Dover sole. We do not yet know the hunger that will take us in its grip. But for now we are perfectly satisfied; like all the other tourists who daily circumnavigate Lucca's terrifying walls, we are quite content. In a few days we are going south, to the house that will be our home until the summer comes. I wonder what awaits us there. I wish I knew better, how to tell the difference between the good and the bad, the truth and the imitation. I wish I could learn how to read the structure of life as weathermen read the structure of clouds, where the future must be written, if only you knew what to look for.

THE PREGNANT MADONNA

The Pregnant Madonna lives in the village, beside the main road. They keep her in the old schoolhouse. It is a small, plain, white cement building, distinct from the precarious earth-colored terraces that form silent, dark, delicate chasms around the narrow village streets, winding uphill to their own exiguous and mysterious summit. The village suffered an earthquake in 1917, in which the original school building was destroyed. We meet an elderly lady who tells us how on that day her throat was sore and her mother let her stay at home. More than half of her classmates were killed by the building's collapse. These days the school is situated in a modern complex elsewhere and the small, vaguely funereal, white cement building that extemporized between tragedy and renewal houses the Madonna.

On that side of the village the road, leading nowhere in particular, is quiet. Once or twice a day an air-conditioned coach appears at the narrow intersection like a vast, snub-nosed whale, venting great sighs from its hydraulic brakes, and clumsily maneuvers itself into place outside the old school. From its side tourists are disgorged, people from Germany and Holland, people from Japan, come to unearth the Madonna from her obscurity here by the side of the road. The rest of the time the building stands brilliant white and silent in the sunshine while the curator sits on the

front steps, reading the *Corriere della Sera* and smoking Marlboro
Lights. He is a man with business interests, and has dogs that are
reputed to be the most voracious truffle hunters in the region. Often a woman is sitting on the steps in his place, keying messages on
her mobile phone or talking over the little gardens to the lady who
runs the café a few doors up. There are quite a few women prepared to keep an eye on the Madonna for the truffle hunter. I
often pass the old school and see one or another of them, half
bored, half dreaming, suspended somehow in her posture there on
the steps, and they seem to me to have a certain kinship with the
Madonna herself, with her weary pregnant slouch and her ambivalent mouth. Not so long ago the Metropolitan Museum of Art
in New York offered three million euros for her, and the Italian
government paid the ransom. At five o'clock the truffle hunter or
one of his molls locks the little wrought-iron gate at the bottom of
the steps and knocks off for the day, pocketing the key and wandering away down the quiet road that is half shadow, half light.

　　We are staying not far away, in a house up a steep dirt track on
top of the facing hill, with a kilometer or so of intricate Italian
fields in between and a soft green valley on the other side. This
house is to be *casa nostra* for the next two months. We arranged it
all in England, not knowing what we would find. I saw photographs of it, as I saw photographs of many other houses, photographs that filled me with strange feelings of voyeurism: pictures
of rooms with enormous three-piece suites, of knickknacks and
blackened fireplaces, of strangers' beds and kitchens and bath-
rooms, all suffused with an atmosphere of sadness, of imperma-
nence, as though the people who lived there had been lost or gone
astray. By contrast, the photographs of our house were so subtle as
to reveal virtually nothing about it at all. They were studies of light
and shade and perspective, abstract and beautiful. If only in mat-

ters of taste, I felt sure that the person who had taken them could be relied on.

The house is near Arezzo, on the eastern edge of Tuscany, where a road continues east through a gorge whose steep wooded sides plunge down on either side from far overhead. The road winds on and on through this green chasm-like wilderness. When it comes out, it is onto the flattest of plains. It is this proximity of extremes that gives the Italian landscape its atmosphere of minia-

turism. It is like traveling through the plaster contour maps that
hung on the wall of our geography room at school and that always
seemed so enchanting, with their cozy little woods, their baby hills
and streams, their gnomish dwellings and small, scaleable mountains. In the distance a village stands as though on an island, its
shining roofs and tower crowning a mound of hill that rises alone
out of the flat terrain. Beyond it are purple hills of an unearthly
appearance, dreamlike and remote, as unreachable as the distances of a painting. The large soft sky rolls with cloud: the light
falls in columns on the flat fields. The road goes up through the village with its deep, narrow streets and out the other side. Now it
runs among hills, orderly and wavelike and neatly cultivated, with
stone houses and ancient castellated towers in the folds.

There is something almost comical about them: they are so
childlike and undulating and miniature, so picturesque and unreal. There is a sign by the roadside that reads *Umbria*, but our
house is not in Umbria. The road goes there, meanders away
and disappears into its green wooded hills. At the same place there
is another sign, small and hand-painted, that points right. It
reads *Fontemaggio*. A dirt track threads its way across the fields and
up a hill, at the top of which stands a house. In the late afternoon
the light suddenly ebbs away from the wave-like hills. I was to
notice this often, how night fell in the valley, not through the arrival of darkness but through the departure of light. The darkness
has no substance: it is merely an absence, a suspension. At this
time of day the house makes a black shape on its lonely hilltop. Its
silhouette is imposing, and far from friendly. We look at it from
down below: we seem, all of a sudden, so far from home, so self-
willed and rootless. And yet it is this feeling that is the decisive
stroke in the process of our liberation. As we look at those dark,
distant windows our bounds are cut, our anchors weighed. We

turn the car off the road and creep slowly into the quiet of the lightless fields.

∞

There is a bang at the door. It is a man. He is wearing an anorak with a hood, for it is raining, though so softly that it is more like mist. His name is Jim: he introduces himself, with handshakes all round, and distributes his card. I look at it. It says: *Enjoy a drink! Jim Balercino, Scottish Taxi Service.* For a moment I misunderstand it, for it seems to suggest that it is Jim who will be offering drinks to his passengers, and that that is what a Scottish taxi service is. In fact I am a little disconcerted generally by his arrival, with his broad Dundee accent and his anorak. It gives substance to my fear that this landscape is inhabited entirely by foreigners, all tussling over their threadbare scrap of Italian culture. I have found one or two paperbacks in the sitting room, with titles like *Extra Virgin* and *Tuscany for Beginners* ("Love and War in a Hot Climate!"), which I feel certain our gracious owner must have allowed to remain there either ironically or by mistake.

But Jim has not come to tout for business. He has come to make sure that we are all right. The telephone number on his card is for our own personal use, should we find that we are not all right. He lives just over there, on the opposite hill, where this morning, looking out of our window, we saw what the darkness had hidden from us the night before: a great castle, with a village at its feet. That is the village where Jim lives. It stands on its hill and we stand on ours, and the valley floor lies in between, a distance of perhaps five hundred meters as the crow flies, though Jim, of course, lives in Umbria and we do not. He has lived here for fourteen years. This does interest me, if only in the context of *Italian in Three Months.* I wonder how well he speaks it: I imagine his

Dundee accent sitting on his tongue, as stubborn as a stain. I am
enthralled by the prospect of his fluency, for fluent he must be, after all this time. But Jim claims not to speak any Italian at all. He
understands a bit, he says, but he can't really speak it. He stands
there in the hall, reiterating that we must ask him for whatever we
need. He's a sort of unofficial minder, he says, for the Brits that
come to the area. He chucks the children under their chins. But he
seems a little mystified by us nonetheless. No one has ever rented
this house for such a long period, he says. Usually they just stay a
week or two. Before he leaves, he tells us that on Sunday nights, at
the bar in his village, there is some kind of festivity. He calls it
"cha-cha": I have no idea what it is, but I don't doubt that it will
be a breeding ground for Jim's pet Brits. Mildly, he exhorts us to
come. The kids'll enjoy it too, he says, chucking them again. Sunday night is tomorrow. I am determined not to go: I would rather
spend a whole evening studying the agreement of the past par-
ticiple with the direct object pronoun. I would rather spend the
evening reading *Extra Virgin*.

In the afternoon it rains harder. We can't turn the heating on
and the house is cold. A pall of wet gray mist hangs over the valley. The castle looks somber and beautiful, in its shroud of mist
and rain. After a while the rain stops and the others go out for
a walk. I remain at home to investigate the *proprietario*'s library.
There are a great many books about Renaissance art. I turn their
pages; I glance at their Madonnas and Crucifixions, their Annunciations and Resurrections; I probe their texts a little and turn
again. I feel that I am standing on the edge of an ocean of knowledge. It is a beautiful ocean, and not uninviting, but all the same it
requires my complete immersion in a new element. I don't know
how to start; I don't know where to breach these waters. I pick up
a little book about Piero della Francesca, for there is a print of one

of his paintings hanging in a frame in the hall. Straightaway I see names that are familiar to me, Arezzo and Sansepolcro, and even the name of our own village on its island in the plain. There is something called the Piero della Francesca Trail, and it appears to run right past our door. I imagine it as an actual path, zigzagging its way across the fields. I read that Piero was born five miles away, in Sansepolcro, in 1410. His mother was born in our village: that is why the *Madonna del Parto* is here. There is a print of it in the

Madonna del Parto, c. 1450–70, by Piero della Francesca (c. 1415–92)

book. I am startled by it: it is like no Madonna that I have seen before in my life. What a strange expression she wears; what an abstracted, ambivalent look. It is a look that has been known, not imagined. It is a look that I am surprised to see on a human face. Such things as it expresses were not, I thought, visible to the eye.

It is raining again. The water batters hard on the roof; I look out of the window and see it falling in swaths across the valley. I run outside with my arms full of coats and umbrellas, meaning to go and find the others, and discover them standing on the front porch. A car is disappearing down the drive: it is Jim's taxi. He has just brought them home. They were walking up through the valley. They were in his village when it started to rain.

The children are beside themselves, wanting to tell the story. It seems they took shelter under a stone *loggia* at the front of a beautiful house in the village square. They are standing under this *loggia* when the front door opens and a lady invites them inside. She leads them through great marble-floored rooms into her kitchen, where a fire is lit and there are children sitting around a big table. They are invited to join them: their clothes are dried before the fire; they are given drinks, and things made out of chocolate, things so delicious that they are unable fully to describe them to me. This lady, Paola, lives in Florence with her husband and children, but in the holidays they come here, to her childhood home. Outside, the rain has become a torrent. Paola wonders how her visitors are to return to Fontemaggio, and they mention that they met a taxi driver called Jim. Perhaps they could use her phone to call him. Paola laughs. There is no need to call: Jim lives here. He rents the top floor of the house, with its beautiful views of the hills toward Arezzo. They go up the stairs and there's Jim, watching a tennis match on television. The children are amazed. Immediately he dons his anorak to take them home. He will accept no payment. They should see it as a favor.

"Cha-cha" it is: Jim is our hero; I am unanimously overruled. It transpires that it is *ciaccia*, not a dance but a food, the traditional Sunday night repast of Italian families. The bar is far up a steep hillside, on the road that leads from Jim's village into the mountains. Everyone is indoors because of the cold. Outside, big puddles make dark shapes on the concrete floor of the deserted terrace. Inside it is brilliant yellow with electric light. Jim is sitting at a long crowded table like the tables you see in paintings of the Last Supper. He knows everyone. He stops and talks with the old toothless men in their berets, with the round women in their gold earrings and dainty shoes, with the witty *padrone* and with his proud daughter who works behind the bar. Men with Giotto faces clap him on the shoulder as they pass. I see that he looks more than a little Italian himself, with his brown eyes and small, well-modeled head, his dapper tucked-in shirt. The anorak was deceiving. And as for all this talk, it does not pour forth in the argot of the Highland Glens, though I can see why Jim resiled from giving a true account of his Italian. A true account of it would be hard to give. There are only two things to be said about it: that it is mechanically sound; and that in no part or article of it is his Dundee brogue compromised.

We are introduced to everyone at the table. They are an assortment, of foreigners and locals and people from Sansepolcro, Piero's hometown. There are the couple who live in the castle and the gay antiques dealer and the man from Milan who makes classical guitars by hand. There is Tiziana, the village beauty. There is a woman from Florida who has immigrated to Italy with her two children, and the woman's sister, who lives in Chicago and has a holiday house in the valley. The two Americans are called Laurie and Suzanne. Laurie is small and neat and slim. Her sister has beautiful milk-white skin like a baby's that sits in folds at her neck and her wrists. She wears her dark hair in curls, and is abundantly groomed and perfumed and painted. Laurie is a little wizened and anxious-looking. Her children, two girls of eight and thirteen, sit beside her and glance at her frequently. Laurie and Suzanne are Jewish. They say they are the only Jews in the area. They shot the rest, Laurie says drily. They did it in the field right opposite my house. I can see the place from my kitchen window. Together they laugh. Suzanne says people here are always asking her if she knows about the Jewish cemetery. There is a Jewish cemetery in the village. She supposes they are just trying to be friendly, but it happens two or three times a week.

The *ciaccia* comes: it is two triangular slices of pizza sandwiched together. Laurie's daughters have theirs with Nutella inside. The younger one takes two delicate bites and pushes it away. Laurie rolls her eyes. *Mangia come un uccello*, she tells the table. Her Italian is a Jewish-American hybrid of Jim's. The girl nods sadly. I eat like a bird, she says. She reveals that her name is Harley. Her father named her, after his motorbike. I notice that Laurie and Suzanne are exchanging significant looks. You're doing it again, Suzanne says to her, *sotto voce*. Laurie opens her eyes wide. Am I? she mouths. Suzanne nods. You're doing it again, she repeats. We talked about this earlier and now you're doing it again. Laurie gives a little anxious placatory grimace and turns brightly away to talk to someone else.

Jim admits that Tiziana is his girlfriend. They have been together for three years. She is down at the other end of the table, tossing her mane like a restless filly, flashing her eyes at him. He tells us that she is forty-three. She wants to move in with him. She wants to put an end to the tennis-watching, to the Brit-minding. She wants to marry him and have children. Jim sits with his hands clasped prayerfully around his glass. I'm not having any of that, he says. He shakes his head. Our relationship, he says ponderously, is as stale as an old piece of Tuscan bread.

∞

It rains for ten days. Jim procures the key to the room under the house where the firewood is kept. He tells us that there were three Irish couples staying here just before we came. They were cold too. It seems they only stayed a week. They were hugely fat, he says, each pair bigger than the last. At the end of the week the cleaners found empty bottles everywhere, boxes of them to be taken away. I suppose they kept themselves warm that way, he says.

The Italians, apparently, are distraught about the weather. They have never known its like before. It isn't their tourists they're worried about: it is their vineyards and their harvests. In the fields around our house, whole families work together on their land, hoeing their rows of green shoots. I see a bent old woman on a hillside in a head scarf and apron, furiously digging at the flinty earth with a trowel in her hand. I see old men driving ancient tractors, holding umbrellas over their heads. It is curious to see these sights, so foreign to the English countryside. I grew up in East Anglia, where combine harvesters rolled like tanks over denuded fields as vast and flat as oceans, and the elderly watched television in well-heated retirement homes. These activities in the fields bear a distinct cast of ambition. I have already noticed that the Italians are unusually enterprising in the uses they make of their lot. There's a metalworker in the village who Jim tells us has just been given the contract to make the doors for the new Wembley Stadium.

∝

We go to Sansepolcro in the rain. It lies in the direction of the strange purple hills, across the plain where factories and super-markets and car showrooms line the road, for Sansepolcro is no longer the one-horse town that Aldous Huxley discovered in its dusty obscurity as an early pilgrim on the Piero della Francesca Trail. Like other places, it has elected to keep its beautiful heart beating with an ersatz modern apparatus of hideous ugliness. We shelter from the rain in the Museo Civico. There are people in here, tourists, though of a superior kind. They pass through the rooms quietly, in groups. They are mostly of late middle age, and well turned-out: there are no giant khaki shorts and tennis socks here, no baseball caps or long lenses. These people have expensive jewelry and leather handbags and polished shoes. They stand in front of one painting after another while their guide lectures them in dispassionate global English. They like to be lectured, it is clear. Their bright eyes pay attention; their lipsticked mouths do not move. They have a look of health about them, as though they were receiving some rigorous but beneficent cure. They are art lovers: it is culture that is purifying their blood and keeping their spines so straight.

When Huxley finally made it to Sansepolcro, after ten hours on a potholed dirt road, he found Piero's *Resurrection* and an-nounced it to be the world's greatest painting. Perhaps, after his long and difficult journey, he felt a little as though he had painted it himself. The *Resurrection* hangs here, in the Museo Civico. I have been reading Vasari's *Lives of the Artists* and have learned some-thing of Piero's obscurity, his lost works and lost reputation, his

mathematical theories of perception and the blindness in which he passed the last twenty years of his life. "Admittedly," Vasari says, "time is said to be the father of truth, and sooner or later it reveals the truth; nevertheless, it can happen that for some while the one who has done the work is cheated of the honour due to him." That is true enough, in life as well as art; but in life, which in general leaves no trace behind it, no object through which the reassessment can be made and the belated honor granted, the

one who has done the work must sometimes be satisfied with
the work itself. And that, perhaps, is what Piero did. He did not
move to Florence or to Rome, like other artists: he stayed here
and was an officer on the town council. His house, apparently, was
decorated from floor to ceiling in every room with wondrous frescoes painted by his own hand. But after his death it was destroyed,
like so much of his work, for it seems that when people destroy
things they do not always know what it is they are destroying. And
perhaps it was Piero's fault that he lacked the vanity to defend his
own creations. There is something in his paintings that is not entirely of this world. He wrote a great many mathematical books,
of which the paintings might be said to be the workings-out. A
fragment from Piero's house still survives, an image of Hercules
clad in the lion's skin, the lion's tail dangling between his legs. It
is a little piece of paganism in the Renaissance ocean of Christian iconography. It is said to be a self-portrait. The lion's paws
are neatly tied over Hercules' groin. His face is full of solitude
and separation. In his hand he holds a thick stick, his weapon
against the world, against its irrationality, its dangers both real and
imaginary.

I can see the *Resurrection* over the heads of the art lovers. Even
from this distance it is surprising: it is startling as the violation of
spatial laws by a human body is always startling. When a person
stands too close to you, you can feel fear, intimacy, oppression,
deep forms of love. This is what Piero's Christ does. The painting
can barely hold him in. He is barefoot, emerging from his tomb.
The art lovers move away a little and the lower half of the painting is disclosed. I see that he is not quite as peremptory as I
thought. There are people in front of him, men, lolling against the
tomb. They are asleep: he is awake. He is fenced in behind them.
He is the victim, after all. He looks straight ahead. He wears a dis-

quieting expression of terrible knowledge. The art lovers murmur and move next door. The rain falls outside the windows of the Museo Civico.

Hercules, c. 1475 (fresco), by Piero della Francesca

∽

Along the road to Arezzo, prostitutes stand in the lay-bys and wait for the lorries to pull over. There is no motorway crossing Tuscany from east to west and so all the freight traffic comes along the single-carriage road that winds down from the hills toward Siena and the plain. At the Arezzo turnoff we pass the Hotel Piero della Francesca, a forlornly hideous roadside edifice, and a little later, toward the center of town, the multistory concrete Parking Piero della Francesca.

The sky is bright and clear and blue. The sun is strong: it makes sharp, dark wedges of shadow in the narrow streets. In the parks the trees cast their filigree shapes on the grass. The stone piazzas and the churches bask in light. We make our way through busy avenues of smart shops and restaurants. We do not linger: we are on the Piero della Francesca Trail, which does not cross the portals of boutiques and pizzerias and souvenir shops. Up a narrow little alleyway there is a small quiet square with a small plain church in it. This church is nothing like as grand as others we've passed along the way. It is hard to believe that we are in the right place. We open the door and go into its cold and gloom-filled interior. A man immediately asks us for our tickets. We have no tickets: we must go and purchase them at the office next door. At the office it seems that we must make an appointment. The frescoes are not to be approached casually: it has to be arranged. Fortunately there is a space an hour hence. We buy our tickets and leave.

Out in the little square we sit on the fountain and eat ice creams. After an hour has passed we go back into the church. We show our tickets and are permitted to go inside. It is much larger than it looks from the outside, and so dark that the walls lie in deep tents of shadow. They are covered with dim forms. Are these our

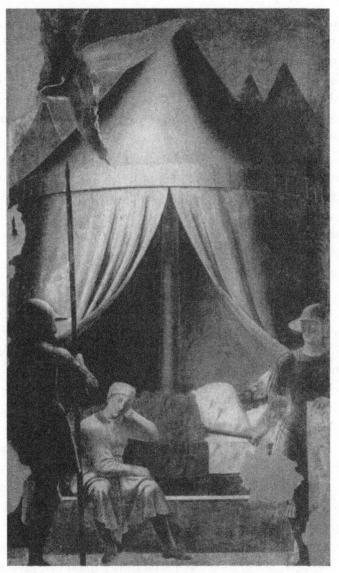

The Dream of Constantine, from *The Legend of the True Cross* cycle, completed 1464 (fresco), by Piero della Francesca

frescoes? We go closer: they are so strange and faded and damaged that they can barely be seen. It is disappointing. An official approaches us: we are not meant to stop here. We are to go there, down toward the altar at the far end of the church. There is a roped-off enclosure there and a large curtain and another official who studies our tickets and looks at his watch. At the appointed moment he lets us in.

The fresco cycle of the Capella Maggiore took Piero ten years to complete. It seems that he worked with extraordinary slowness, though the technique itself is immediate and quick-setting. I think of his sympathetic image of Hercules and wonder whether painting was in truth a terrible labor for Piero, an agonizing process of atonement, of putting right. He would apply wet cloths to the plaster at night so that he could work two days on a single section. His preparatory drawings and calculations took even longer than the painting itself, for he was always the mathematician. He would seem to want to persuade you that these two callings are one, to show you only what is eternal. Not what is explanatory or circumstantial or even real, but what is always and forever true.

He did not, I think, trouble himself over their subject matter, which is the Legend of the True Cross. This saga, which purports to tell of how the tree that grew from Adam's body became the cross upon which Christ was crucified, is without doubt the religious story that makes its way most tortuously through human affairs. It features everyone from Cain and Abel to the Queen of Sheba. It features crusades and visions, evangelism and politics and unsavory forms of Christian heroism. Yet entering the rectangular bay of the Capella for the first time is like passing from darkness into light; like looking out from a wintry room to a garden in summer, to blue sky and sunlight and trees. It is like emerging from imprisonment or blindness, and remembering what the world is really like.

∝

I dream that my husband returns from town with armfuls of clothes that he has bought, fitted clothes in beautiful colors like the clothes Piero's women wear, with intricate sleeves and pearl buttons. I presume they are for me and I see his surprise: clearly they are meant for our daughters, though he doesn't say it and allows me to try them. One after another I try to put them on. They are all too small. The little pearl buttons won't do up. My arms strain and tear the delicate sleeves.

In the Capella Maggiore there is a painting of the Emperor Constantine dreaming. How can such a thing be painted? Piero shows Constantine asleep, in a tent. The folds are parted to reveal him there, his eyes closed. The tent is so clear and firm, so tall and shapely and richly colored, with the dim figure of Constantine inside. Though it is night, there is a strong light falling on its folds. The tent is the dream, more substantial than the dreamer. I wonder whether it is when we sleep that we are truly awake. As a child I entertained this fear: how beloved the concrete world seemed then, how horrible the lawlessness of dreams. There is an angel above Constantine's tent: it is telling him that he must fight his enemy Maxentius in the name of the cross if he wishes to defeat him. This battle is waged across the adjacent wall, on horseback amid a bristling forest of lances. Above is the limpid, duck-egg-blue Sansepolcro sky, and in the background a little river meanders eternally through the green Tuscan fields like a ribbon of light, three tiny white birds afloat on its glassy surface.

It is only by craning my neck that I notice the image in the

The Death of Adam, from *The Legend of the True Cross* cycle, completed 1464
(fresco), by Piero della Francesca

Capella that afterward I think of most. It is in the top right-hand
lunette, a portrait of Eve as an old woman, attending Adam at his
death. It is another mathematical truth, but of a different kind.
She stoops in a dreary gray dress. Her wrinkled breasts sag. Her
face wears that look so characteristic of the elderly, an expression
of preoccupation with inalterable things. Her hand rests on her
husband's shoulder.

∞

In the garden of the house the green geckos speed along cracks
in the walls; the ants fulminate in their patches, carrying shreds
of leaf like little sails that tilt and curve, winding through the dirt

and grass. The days are warm now. Around the wisteria the bees steadily drone and sketch their vague sweeping lines through the air. Caterpillars inch their way across vast expanses of paving stone, workmanlike, determined, and once I see a gecko dart out from a rock and, at the end of its long journey, snatch the furry body in its jaws and carry it away.

Madonna of Senigallia with Child and Two Angels, c. 1470
(tempera on panel), by Piero della Francesca

One day we go to Urbino, the last stop on the Piero della
Francesca Trail. There are no queues in Urbino: the road is too
winding, the location too remote. In the empty Galleria Nazionale
we find Piero's *Madonna di Senigallia*, austere, gray, full of a cold
northern light. It is a painting whose subject is purity, but it also
seems to me to be some kind of statement. It is as if the artist is no-
tifying us that he is withdrawing from the things of this world. In
the background the light slants forever through the slatted window.
The Madonna and her companions are silent, abstracted. The
baby holds a white flower. The plain, pewter-colored room contains them in its unadorned eternity. Yet they seem, somehow, to
be taking their leave.

There is a meeting in the village in protest at the government's
plans to build a motorway east through the valley. The intricate,
ancient vista, Piero's vista, will be destroyed. An English lady is
tearful at the prospect. Jim consoles her. Ach, it'll take them years,
he says. By the time they do it we'll all be old and gray. It won't
make any difference to us.

I have understood, I think, Piero's message, though its tidings
are not of joy. It is at once more rational than joy and more beautiful. It is that you must seek a truth that lies beyond human concerns. I keep this with me as the days pass. The white birds on the
water; the light slanting through the window. The man rising from
his tomb, full of a terrible knowledge.

THE CASTLE

The children look at the castle across the valley. In the mornings we sit with them on the terrace doing schoolwork. We do maths, long pages of sums which they complete in their spidery handwriting. We do painting. We read aloud. The castle stands there, mystical and golden, its crenellations etched in shadow, and every so often they glance up at it. By now its romance is more real to them than their maths. They spring up from the table and run off to climb the cherry tree in the garden.

The castle is tall and thick and square: it is how I imagine Fabrizio's tower to have been in Stendhal's *Charterhouse of Parma*. During his escape Fabrizio encountered certain problems caused by natural characteristics the building had acquired over time. Forests of gorse grew from its sides; it bulged and fell away unpredictably, had patches that were slippery as ice and others that were rough and so jagged they would cut the skin. Originally the production of man, the tower was reverting to nature, or acquiring a nature of its own. And indeed the village *castello* has something not human about it, despite its driveway and flower beds and swimming pool. A narrow road runs all the way around its perimeter, abutting the walls. From our house across the valley the walls look beautiful and soft, but close up they are as sheer and merciless as cliffs.

Jim, of course, is on terms of the utmost familiarity with the *castello*'s inhabitants. He comes and goes beneath those precipitous walls as blithely as he might cross the threshold of an overheated bungalow in suburban Dundee. He is keen for us to have a look inside. He's got us down as the sightseeing type. He mentions a room in the *castello* where there are frescoes, and then looks at us out of the corner of his eye, as though half expecting us to land on him in a body and tear him limb from limb in our excitement. For several days this visit is uppermost in Jim's mind. Every time he sees us he mentions it, with increasing testiness, for having decided we ought to be given a tour of the *castello* it is not apparent to him why this should not occur immediately. The family agreed to a time, he says, and then phoned to cancel it. He suggested another time and they haven't yet got back to him. He doesn't know what the problem is. He refers to personal difficulties for which it is clear his reserves of patience have run dry. Such human entanglements contravene the laws of Jim's obliging universe, where the smoothing of paths and the offer of a helping hand are as inviolate as the sun and moon, or ought to be. I have noticed that Jim has quite a grand manner in the prosecution of this system. Its values are entirely social: their notions of right and wrong have no moral basis at all. His codes of conduct all grow from a single root, which is the protection of interests. For reasons which are unclear to me, the standoff at the *castello* is running directly counter to the interests of all concerned, not least those of the owners themselves.

In Italy, gossiping, even of a scandalous kind, is a morally neutral activity; emotions, except as they force the hand of politics, are a public spectacle, like the opera. And like the opera they can engage our pity, our humor, our love of beauty and truth: they are greatly respected, but theirs is not the deciding vote in the judgment of human activities. Interests, and what advances or impairs them, are all. Jim is always willing to make an example of Tiziana, and he does so now. Tiziana's interests and his own are fundamentally opposed. Three years ago she returned to the village after a period away. She had married, but the marriage quickly failed; she had lived in Spain for a while, worked as a teacher, moved here and there, but nothing had come of it. So she came back, and moved in with her mother, who lived alone. Tiziana has built a wooden hut in the garden and that is where she resides. Nothing could better symbolize how temporary she intends her solitary state to be than this frail wooden hut; and nothing could better express the pent-up force of frustration that rages in her breast than the two giant, lavishly furred black dogs she keeps there, smothering them with a strange, suggestive care and kissing their snapping, sharp-toothed muzzles.

Jim, on the other hand, married very young and had a child. His wife was Italian, from Rome. Jim is half-Italian himself, which accounts both for his looks and for his sense of social intrigue. His grandparents came to Dundee as immigrants from a village in Liguria, and built an ice cream factory which his father and now his brother continue to manage. Jim does not say much about the success or otherwise of this enterprise, but one day, in his apartment, he bashfully shows us a photograph of the family seat in Scotland, a vast aristocratic dwelling of considerable beauty and grandeur in whose vicinity for one reason or another Jim does not choose to live. Jim's young wife moved to London with him; their son was born; Jim, by his own account, did not treat her well. She was homesick and lonely, and he was restless and disloyal. Eventually she left him and brought up the child alone. She has earned his respect over the years. He regrets the way he treated her. It was a great mistake. His son has been well educated and is now grown up. He is a good lad, good-looking and intelligent, and devoted to his mother. Jim, when he sees him, is reminded of some incapacity in his own nature that has been the chief source of pain in his experience of life. He doesn't know what it is, only that it is there. And that his bachelor existence is both the expiation of it and the unique form of its relief. His top-floor flat is his sanctuary; and his retirement from the battlefield of married life, injured but not fatally so, is the piece of good luck on which he intends to last out his days.

It might be said that Jim is harming Tiziana's interests by allowing her to cherish her hopes of him. He should let her go, and God knows he's tried to get rid of her. They have often separated, but they always seem to drift back together again.

As for the denizens of the *castello*, well, they are the last in a line that extends unbroken across two centuries, though this epoch is now well advanced into twilight. The old man, Gianni, is on his last legs: his two daughters, both in their late forties, are childless. They are both married, but they continue to live in the *castello* with their father. The elder daughter lives a life of solitary, aristocratic dignity, doing good works in the village, riding her horses, and advancing her studies of literature. She has the upright, unself-pitying demeanor of a nun. I often see her striding about in jodhpurs and long leather riding boots and once or twice she has accosted me, wanting to talk about poetry, or an English novel she is trying to translate into Italian.

Her sister's husband is Alfredo, a close associate of Jim's. Their friendship is the perfect expression of Jim's theories of social practice. Alfredo is a corpulent, slow-moving individual with a large, rough-skinned, pitted face of quite exceptional malevolence and dissipation. His small eyes look out of it with an expression of mingled torpor and amusement, like that of a boa constrictor who has just swallowed something large, and whose pleasant recollections of the event give way now and then to the sleepiness of a full stomach. He is often to be seen behind the tinted windows of a new silver Audi, slowly cruising the lanes and byways of the village, before disappearing back to Pistoia, where, according to Jim, he has a house. His visits to the village are territorial, like those of a shark cruising its habitual waterways. Once, we are walking along the unfrequented road back to Fontemaggio when the silver Audi glides quietly past and then draws to a halt just ahead with the engine running. The electric window slides down: there is Alfredo, leering at us from inside. He salutes us vaguely with his fat hand, on which he wears several heavy rings. *Va bene?* he says. *Tutto bene?* He looks us up and down. He grins. So, he says, you are coming to see my house. *Casa mia.* We realize he is referring to the *castello.* We say that we don't know, that Jim mentioned something, that everyone is very busy. He shrugs and grins again lazily and the darkened glass slides up in front of his face. Jim lives in fear of a summons to spend the evening with Alfredo: these are frequent, and put him out of action for a week afterward.

Our invitation to the *castello* comes. The *signorina* meets us on the driveway, in severe riding habit and boots. She shows us her pet tortoises, who stumble around a fenced enclosure on the front lawn. Their wrinkled gray necks and blindly searching heads seem so vulnerable, protruding from their indestructible shells. She has other pets too, donkeys and goats and sheep she has rescued over the years. She keeps them in the stables, where the carriages used to be.

Other people arrive: Suzanne, the rotund American, and a couple from Milan. A car careers at breakneck speed into the driveway and Tiziana springs forth from its front seat, teeth bared and mane flying. The old man, Gianni, comes slowly toward us along a gravel path. His shoulders are bent; his head is fragile-looking, the skin a thin tissue threaded with veins, the eyes watery and depthless like a new baby's. Yet his bones are large: they stand like the posts and beams of a ruined house amid its decaying walls and roof. We are led inside, into a great hall as cold and bare as a monastery. The *signorina* talks: we follow her up a grand stone staircase, through empty rooms where the light slants undisturbed across the flagstones. In one room there is a pigeon. The *signorina* explains that it lives there. It is one of her protégés: it had a broken wing. Shortly afterward we come to the frescoes: they decorate another empty room, to whose old varnished boards they impart a haunted atmosphere, for they remain bright and florid in the desolation, their scenes and figures unfaded. The *signorina* tells us they have been restored, lavishly so. No expense was spared. They have, themselves, no great distinction: the distinction lies in what they are, for in Italy art is no longer permitted to die a natural death. People would say it was a shame if the *castello* did not take care of its frescoes.

On the next floor, things change: this is the domain of Alfredo. We enter an elegant room with a great window and a lordly marble fireplace. The window has a view of the mountains behind the village. We went up there one day, and found a whole ghost settlement at the top, a place that no road leads to any longer. We walked in the overgrown cemetery and along the hollowed-out main street. The gardener at Fontemaggio tells us that his grandmother used to go every week to the market there. She lived in Arezzo, and would walk all night across the mountains with her cows and her produce to buy and sell. The distance was twenty kilometers. She left in the early evening and arrived at dawn.

In front of the window stands Alfredo's desk. This is his study. He is an architect: there is a framed certificate hanging on the wall. This room was created for him, in the hope that it might inspire him to work. The desk is made of polished engraved wood. It is a whole hand thick, and as big as a bed. Its surface is beautifully laid out, with fountain pens and compasses and drawing materials, all new. There is a block of unmarked paper and an empty leather chair, with its back facing the window. We pass into a sort of modern apartment, a vast room that extends the whole width of the castle, with leather sofas and low glass tables, sculptures in metal and wood, canvases and expensive lamps and books, and a whole glass wall that overlooks the valley. Jim regards this spectacle with a jaded air: this is where his evenings with Alfredo usually commence. There is an opulent bathroom next door, lined with marble from floor to ceiling like a tomb, and a bedroom with a black leather bed. Alfredo is apparently willing to rent this apartment to tourists. Suzanne says he has asked her to recruit victims from among her American acquaintances, but the rent is so high that nobody she knows can afford it.

Alfredo's kingdom comes to an end: we go up, up a steep staircase and then up an even steeper one, and then up another, narrow and made of wood. Gianni follows all the way, arthritic but resolute. Tiziana holds the children's hands, clutching at them with her long painted fingernails, shrieking concerned injunctions against falling, and flashing triumphant looks at Jim's impervious back when she succeeds in getting them to the top unharmed. Finally, we come to a tiny door that lets us out onto the castle parapets. There is a narrow walkway all the way round. On one side is the castle roof; on the other is empty air. We file out. There below are the wavelike undulating hills, the village on its mound, the pale road that lies on the valley floor like a length of ribbon. There, opposite, is Fontemaggio, and around it one or two other houses that on the ground are far away, separate and distinct in their own folds of hillside. The view from the top of the *castello* is not larger or more sweeping than the view from the village itself.

It is the sudden effect of height that is unexpected. From above, the dimension of experience is lost, the feeling of involvement shrugged away. The earth goes about its own eternal business, rising and falling, growing or decaying; the late sun slants across it, the trees and houses correspond with their own little shadows. It is difficult from here to imagine time passing in minutes, in hours, to discern the intricacy of life, to distinguish one house from another,

one day from another, one existence from any other. From here, only epochs are visible. We look down on it, as children believe people do from heaven. I do not like this feeling, of being separated from the earth. The soles of my feet prickle: I press myself back against the slant of the roof. I imagine the building tipping and throwing me out over the side into nothingness.

Beside me, Suzanne is conferring with Gianni on the narrow walkway. She is telling him about the plans for the motorway: she attended the meeting in the village, where the details were made known. She shows him exactly where the road will go, where the tunnels will be drilled. It is a tragedy, she says. She is sure corruption has played its part. She speaks slowly: Gianni is perhaps a little deaf. She pantomimes her outrage with angry gesticulating arms. Gianni stands mutely beside her. I see that tears are dropping down his frail cheeks.

ᴏᴧ

Silvio comes once a week to tend the *proprietario*'s garden. He arrives at dawn: we hear him opening the shed where the tools are kept. The light is pink; there is the sound of birdsong. Silvio's rummagings harmonize with the first stirrings of the earth. Later we hear a car passing along the valley, a dog barking, a tractor starting its engine. We hear the clipping sound of secateurs beneath our window, and the hiss of running water.

Silvio is forty or so, light-haired and wiry, with fair freckled skin that turns red in the sun. He has a bald pate, like a monk: it glows, round and red, in the distances of the garden where he stoops at his work. There is something monkish in his demeanor too, a kind of bodily discipline that gives him a hallmark of solitude. When spoken to he is perfectly still and silent, as though measuring his response. One day one of the children falls out of the cherry tree that grows on a ledge over the steep hillside. Silvio appears at the kitchen door, holding her in his arms. *E caduta*, he says.

Jim says that Silvio used to be something of a tearaway. He doesn't really know him, he says, a statement that arouses my interest, for Jim's knowledge tends to encompass everything that is human and compromised and to leave out that which must be approached dispassionately. It is in this same spirit that Jim claims not to know Italian. Jim not knowing Silvio suggests that Silvio knows himself.

Silvio is as hard to corner as the hare that I sometimes see standing proud and alert in the empty garden, that bounds away at the slightest noise. But one day I offer him coffee, and though he looks at me gravely he does not refuse. He takes it *espresso*, in a tiny cup that stands cooling beside him while he works. I watch him deferring his acceptance of my libation, but finally he picks it up and stands drinking it in little sips, looking out over the valley. After that, Silvio and I are friends. There is something about him, an atmosphere of fracture and recovery, an inward knowledge of failure and of resurrection, that emboldens me to practice my Italian. Silvio's talk is easy to understand; his listening, so quiet and spacious, accommodates my clumsy sentences. He tells me that he works for most of the *stranieri* in the area, watering their gardens, cleaning their swimming pools. Their houses are generally empty, or let out. He drives around in his little car, going from one house to another. He cuts the grass and waters the flowers to stop them dying. I imagine these houses, so civilized and deserted, so strenuously maintained in their untenanted perfection. It is curious that Silvio, who has lived here all his life, should be their caretaker. But he is happy to do the work: it allows him to be free. Otherwise he would have to move to the city. I ask him where he lives, and he points to the top of the highest mountain behind the village. It is smoky with cloud, though the valley lies in sun.

I like to talk to Silvio about football, *il calcio*. I have found that this subject lends itself to the amateur linguist, being both primitive and impersonal and revolving around a small number of stable themes. Silvio is more than usually reserved when the conversation takes this turn, though I talk about it anyway. I attribute his reticence to a spiritual source. He seems like the kind of man whose distinctness from the masculine norm would express itself in an indifference to competitive sport. But one day I mention the news that Italy's top team have been relegated as a punishment for corruption, and observe an expression of blenched severity on Silvio's face. He digs with cold precision at the flower beds. It is good, he says finally. Perhaps now the game will be cleansed.

According to Silvio, corruption is a national affliction. The ordinary Italian can have no dignity, no pleasure in life. Everything around him is corrupt, from politics to the postal service. In things that intimately affect him, the Italian has no rights. Take the plans for the motorway: corruption, double-dyed. It is a case of waiting to see which form of corruption outdoes the others. And yet Italy is so beautiful: its art, its churches, its monuments. Have we been to Perugia, to Assisi? He loves these places but he can no longer visit them. To live in a land that is so beautiful and so diseased is a form of torture. That is why Silvio lives on top of a mountain. In his garden there is a special place for meditation. It is necessary, to have such a place. Otherwise your own anger would consume you.

One day Silvio invites us to visit his house. The road winds out of the village and quickly leaves it behind, climbing steeply among forests and turning through vistas of wooded peaks. It is more than ten kilometers from the village to Silvio's house, and all of it is empty wilderness, a silent world of mountains that stand shoulder to shoulder as far as the eye can see. Once or twice we stop and get out. The sun is close overhead; beneath us there are wisps of cloud. The last section of road is so steep and potholed that it is nearly impossible to ascend. We come out on the very summit, where the wind blows and the light is brilliant. There are two houses there. One looks south, over the mountains toward Cortona. The other faces north, toward Arezzo. They are perhaps twenty meters apart. They sit there back to back on their summit, like refuges for two gods, each with its portion of the hemisphere. Silvio's house is the one that faces north. He tells us that for many years the other house belonged to an English writer, a man who became Silvio's dearest friend. At first he came only in the summer, to write his books, but over time he stayed for longer and longer periods, until he was almost always here. His wife ceased to accompany him: at the beginning she liked the house, but after a while she came to hate it. She found the isolation, particularly in the winter, unbearable. And perhaps she feared that she would lose her husband up here, for he was drawn to it by some private compulsion of his own that she felt inclined to challenge by her absences. He and Silvio spent much of their time together, particularly in the evenings, talking. They developed many things in common. Then, last year, the house was sold. The writer went away, back to his wife, and Silvio was left alone.

Silvio's house feels empty. It is sparsely furnished. There is a photograph on the mantelpiece, of a woman and two children, but he does not say whether they are his family. The decorations are plain. His kitchen table is small, with a single chair. He hunts around for more chairs: he opens a box of biscuits that have obviously been bought for the occasion and arranges them on a plate for the children. He tells us about the ghost village that lies nearby, with its forgotten market; and about his grandmother's night walks all across these mountains. Now there is another ghost here, the ghost of his English friend. Later he shows us his garden, which falls away at the end into nothingness. His place of meditation is just there, on the threshold of a great declivity with the purple peaks ranged around it in the distance. Meditation has become fundamental to his way of life. He has conquered many enemies through discipline alone. Six months ago he overcame the last and most stubborn, which was his addiction to cigarettes.

In another part of the garden I am surprised to see a cage with two dogs in it. They bark wildly when they see us and strain at the doors of their enclosure: they are big, vicious-looking animals, but Silvio assures us they would do us no harm. They know who my friends are, he says. They don't attack unless they are provoked. He fondles their rough heads through the bars. It is necessary to have some kind of protection up here, he says. If someone tried to hurt me, they would kill him. He seems to set great store by this idea, yet he has been wounded to the quick by things of whose scent these animals would not have caught the merest trace. All the same, at night he lets them out into the garden and they patrol the boundaries until dawn.

I AM NOTHING, I AM EVERYTHING

Assisi lies an hour away to the southeast. The day is overcast: clouds sag over the plain. Now and again there is a motiveless gust of wind like an outburst of temper across the flat fields that subsides as suddenly as it came. It is Sunday. The great gray drifting sky, so deep overhead and unalleviated, recalls the Sundays of my childhood with their strange double nature of privation and feasting, a character impassable and final in its duality. The week was dead: it passed away somewhere between Mass and Sunday lunch, which between them finished it off, knocked the living daylights out of it with the sacerdotal rod and the Sunday roast. There was no hope given out for Monday, or for Tuesday either. Week after week they led back to the same impasse, the same nullifying conclusion. I still have a Sunday feeling, even now; a feeling that is like a bruise or mark on the skin, that is tender when it is touched.

From far away, the Basilica di San Francesco can be seen, standing on its hill in a tent of cloud. At the front there is a buttress wall, blank and pagan-looking, frightening in its enormity. The building's long, forbidding colonnaded walkway extends from its side, like the huge dark wing of a bird of prey. I am familiar with the giantism of Catholic architecture. At the pilgrim center of Lourdes in France the main square and basilica are so large that they harmonize unexpectedly with the iconography of late capitalism, with the airport terminal and the runway and the shopping mall. And indeed both are determinedly global in their perspective: visitors surrender their separateness at the sheer scale of the enterprise, without protest. It must be imagined that people are pleased to be relieved of their individuality, though that doesn't seem to be the case when disaster strikes. Then it is the impersonal they fear more than anything else.

As we draw near, the Sunday feeling grows stronger, the atmosphere of Catholicism more unmistakable. There are coach parks, scores of them, for it is in the spectacle of mass transportation that these large-scale beliefs like to show their might. We are controlled and directed by traffic police, by zoning, by different-colored signs with numbered boxes. The traffic police wear white gloves. They point and prohibit and occasionally permit. We wait a long time. At last we are given a zone and a number and allowed through. These precautions have not been put in place to marshal admirers of the early frescoes of Giotto, beautiful though they are reputed to be. It is St. Francis who is causing the crush. All that remains of him are the bones that lie in the basilica's cold heart, but it is the bones the coach parties have come for. The mania for the tangible is the predictable consequence of the intangibility of religious belief, though it has always bewildered me that it should be among the relics of the actual that the missing link between faith and reality is sought. At the Catholic convent school I attended, the nuns were forever debating the authenticity of the Shroud of Turin, or the scrolls of Fatima, or the splinters of the true cross that were in ever-increasing circulation around the Catholic world and that put together could have made a hundred crosses. Such things roused their interest as individuals and, I suppose, alleviated the dreary impersonality of their beliefs. They were a form of attention, of love, for these women had given their lives to Jesus and had nothing whatever to show for it. Their love had no object, and in the end any bone or bit of cloth would do, just as a baby needs a blanket or a teddy bear to soothe him in his mother's absences. Once, our class was taken to see the hand of Margaret Clitheroe, which the Order kept preserved in fluid at their convent in York, and those girls who screamed were immediately given detention.

I have been reading about St. Francis. He was not always the poor antimaterialist who befriended the birds: he came from a family of rich Assisi cloth merchants. He was born in 1182, to doting parents who freighted him with their care and their ambition. His mother named him Giovanni, after John the Baptist, for she desired him to be a religious leader; but his father, who was away on business at the time of the birth, changed the name when he returned, furiously asserting that he did not want the child to be signed over to God. He intended him to work in the family business and drove him hard at his studies of Latin and mathematics, but no doubt he approved of his son's popularity and vigorous social appetites too, for these were suitably ungodly pastimes, and besides, ambition is gratified wherever its object finds approval in the world. Francis danced and feasted and passed his nights in riotous style with his aristocratic friends, while by day he studied and worked in his father's shop. One day a beggar came in to ask for money and Francis threw him out, but a feeling of compunction made him go after the man with a bag of coins and beg his forgiveness. Francis's father disapproved of such spiritual melodrama, and his friends ridiculed it.

Sometime later Assisi declared war against neighboring Perugia and Francis immediately enlisted. He was ambitious for knightly glory and prestige: and for escape, too, it would seem, from his parents and their conflicting desires for him. Later this need would take desperate forms, but as yet Francis perhaps be-

lieved that he could free himself by a worldly route. Almost as
soon as he set off he was captured, and was imprisoned for a year.
When he returned to Assisi he was ill and took to his bed. There a
change took place. It expressed itself in a need to give away his
own possessions, a form of behavior that was also the deepest
challenge he could offer to his father's authority.

Francis began to spend his days alone, forlornly wandering in
the countryside around the town. One day he came across a small
church that lay in ruins and believed that he heard a voice telling
him to repair it. More precisely, the voice is said to have ordered
him to "repair my house which has fallen into ruin." Another man
might have acted on this injunction in the grand manner for which
it appears to legislate, but Francis responded by selling some of his
father's cloth without permission and beginning restoration work
on the little church with the proceeds. It is rare for the voice of
God to initiate a direct attack on the property of the human father.
It is as though Francis's God were a projection of himself, a kind
of universal victim ravaged by the world's misunderstanding and
neglect. Perhaps his spirit had been crushed after all, for like a
child his sympathies ever after lay with dumb creatures, with the
birds and bees whose patron saint he became. His father, Pietro,
accused Francis of theft and led him before the bishop. Pietro explained the whole case, the wealth and education from which his
son had profited, the ingratitude his increasingly strange behavior
evinced and the crime in which it had culminated, a crime the
more outrageous for being perpetrated against his own father, to
whom he owed everything, down to the clothes on his back. At
this, Francis committed his final act of rejection: in front of the
bishop he removed all of his clothes and gave them back to his father. What lengths he went to, both to goad and to free himself
from his oppressive parent! To hand back your own clothes is the

prelude to immolation itself, to the giving back of the body that has struggled to be free and failed. And Francis did go on to lead a life of great privation and denial, in which his interest in his new father and patriarch—God—seems to have been more than a little abstracted. His was a pure brand of nihilism that sought only to shield its most abject and defenseless victims from the evil of humankind. At the end of his life he instructed his followers to bury him at a place called Hell's Hill, a bleak tract of land where executions were customarily held. His sufferings from tuberculosis were extreme, and it was during this final illness that he wrote the "Canticle to the Creatures," a love poem to the unpopulated earth, to the sun and wind and water, to a dumb and beautiful Mother Nature whom he idolized for her impartiality, her lack of motive, her generosity that did not enslave, her abundance that was without cause or consequence.

Two years after Francis's death in 1226, the cult of his celebrity was born. He was canonized, and the Pope laid the foundation stone for the basilica on his grave. He who had suffered so bitterly from the tyranny of identity, whose psyche found relief only in the dissolution of ownership and the casting off of material things, whose eyes dwelt for consolation on what was small and beneath notice, was to be pinioned forever beneath the weight of a giant edifice of unparalleled splendor, in a place he had chosen for its lack of prestige, but which was henceforth to invoke the very origins of human aspiration itself and bear the name of Paradise Hill.

Reading Vasari's *Lives of the Artists*, one begins to notice a minor consistency of an unexpected sort. The artists of the Renaissance, almost without exception, profited early in life from their fathers' help in the recognition and exercise of their talents. Michelangelo, it is true, was occasionally beaten for spending his time drawing

when he should have been studying, but by the time he was fourteen his father had changed his tune and apprenticed him at a living wage to the painter Ghirlandaio. But it is mostly the case that
the child-artist, who in other eras was grudgingly received as a
delinquent or an idiot, was in this time and place favored and forwarded, soldered to the world by the paternalistic hand. And perhaps the psychic health of the art of the Renaissance, its confidence
and sociability and insatiable love of humankind, issues from this
prosaic and fundamental source.

Cimabue, born in 1240, whose works adorn the Basilica of St.
Francis, is credited by Vasari with being the artist who initiated the
great restoration of the art of painting in Italy. At school he would
cover his books with drawings instead of reading them: his parents
congratulated him on his originality. When a group of Greek
craftsmen was brought to Florence to decorate the Gondi Chapel
in Santa Maria Novella, Cimabue truanted school altogether and
spent whole days watching them work. His father approached
these craftsmen and elicited their agreement to take Cimabue on
as an apprentice, for according to Vasari he had a great respect for
his son and believed that his inclinations ought to be trusted. How
different from poor St. Francis, who only had to show an inclination for his father to move to crush it! And how different the pursuit of truth that followed, the one so punitive and painful and the
other so vigorous and beautiful. Cimabue quickly became famous,
so famous that when he painted a large new Madonna for Santa
Maria Novella the painting was processed through the streets to
the sound of trumpets and a cheering crowd. One day, he was
walking in the countryside when he came across a young shepherd
boy sitting in a field, drawing one of his own sheep with a pointed
stone on a smooth piece of rock. This was Giotto. Cimabue was so
astonished by his talent that he asked the boy to come and live

with him, and the boy replied that if his father agreed, then he would. The father was delighted, and Giotto went back with Cimabue to Florence, where, as Vasari admits, he rapidly diminished Cimabue's glory by becoming one of the greatest painters the world has ever known. Dante summed up the situation in the *Divine Comedy*:

> *Once, Cimabue thought to hold the field*
> *In painting; Giotto's all the rage today;*
> *The other's fame lies in the dust concealed.*

It was in the Basilica di San Francesco that these first artists of the Renaissance evolved their artistic vision, for the edifice quickly grew so large that a certain blankness adhered to it, and adheres to it still. It is easy to enlarge the scale of a human construction: what is hard is to amplify its brain. The basilica was a dinosaur that needed to be rendered articulate. That was what the artists were for, to fill in its blankness, to program it with meaning and significance. The modest spirit of St. Francis alone could not fill its barnlike spaces: it required the seasoning of art to flavor the bland atmosphere of pilgrimage.

Yet the modern-day pilgrims like their blandness, their plain fare. The basilica is full of them, passing the painted walls with barely a glance. The specifics of art are too strong for their palates. It is bones they have come for in their air-conditioned coaches; bones, and the experience of their own coming, their massing: the basic unit of life, entire unto itself, moving and massing together like polyps on the ocean bed. Held as they are in the unblinking stare of existence, interpretation and art do not concern them. The painted walls of the basilica are no more to them than the texture of the rock on which their colony has massed itself. Those walls are now faded and damaged with time: they have their own fame, their own divinity, but the pilgrims dislike people looking at paintings. They hiss and shush and send over angry stares. Now and then a message is broadcast over the sound system, reminding those who are not in the basilica to attend Mass that absolute silence is required or they will be asked to leave. Then the voice of the priest singing the liturgy issues from the crackling speakers once more, a sound that is both automatic and animal, like the loud call of some primitive creature whose interminable cadences now and again invite the unanimous caterwauling of his neighbors.

In the upper basilica there are a large number of frescoes depicting the life of St. Francis. Until recently it was believed that Giotto had painted them, but my researches in the *proprietario*'s library have informed me that it is now known that he did not. Nevertheless, his name remains there, in an engraved perspex rectangle on the basilica wall. Elsewhere in the basilica there are works by Cimabue, Simone Martini, Lorenzetti, and the real Giotto, and none of them are labeled at all. They are difficult to find: they lie in sepulchral darkness among the vaults of the lower church, like prisoners in a dungeon. The customary modern appurtenances of the art lover are nowhere to be found. There are no lights, no silken tasseled ropes, no information. One is obstructed and put off the scent at every opportunity. The broadcast warnings intensify: the shushing and the hostile stares come thick and fast through the gloom, for it is in the lower church that the bones lie, and the closer we get to them the more vigorously art is derided.

I begin to feel a little outraged. It is they who seem heretical to me, these spiritual bureaucrats with their rules and regulations, their monotonous chanting, their punitive demeanor and their threats of expulsion. It is they who are insolent: so quick to damn and shame, and glorying so in the execution of it. As a child I was accustomed to the way adults seized on Christianity as a tool, a moralizing weapon they had fashioned in their own subconscious: when they unsheathed it I would glimpse the strange, dark chasm of repression and subjectivity, a place that seemed like a crack in the safe surface of the world; and it did appear to me that judgment lay down there, flowing like a black river within the tributaries of personalities, from a nameless common source. But now I found the Christian story all human, like literature: it was a long time since it had been raised as a weapon over my head. It is perhaps for exactly this reason that the pilgrims object to the Giotto-lovers. The whole place, I now see, has set itself against art as against a rival religion. A group of teenagers with clipboards murmur in front of Lorenzetti's *Madonna dei Tramonti* and are instantly shot down with a volley of glares like a firing squad's fusillade. A child asks a question of its parent concerning Giotto's *Flight into Egypt* and is bludgeoned from all sides with disapproval. They are enraged, these people queuing to worship at the strange, sealed hexagonal tomb. Like Jesus, Francis was a misfit who has become an orthodoxy. But the Pharisee, it seems, was well drawn as an eternal human type. Of what, precisely, are we meant to feel ashamed? Is their faith so fragile, so impacted, that the whole world must be silent while it is teased out? They seem to disapprove so instinctively, as a hand gropes in the darkness for a switch. A little light comes on in their eyes: it reveals something, a sacred space in the brain that perhaps otherwise they would have had trouble finding their way to, with a bone lying in it on a little heap of dust.

In the right wing of the transept there is a famous painting of St. Francis by Cimabue. He is small, hunched, unsmiling. He

St. Francis (fresco), by Cimabue (Cenni di Pepo) (c. 1240–c. 1301)

wears a monk's tonsure and brown cassock and clutches a Bible in
his hands. His eyes are large, almond-shaped, heavy-lidded, of a
light brown color: their expression is unutterably sad. It is not the
sadness that shows in the rolling whites of a saint's upturned, im-

ploring gaze. It is a sadness that you see in the eyes of people who
were unhappy children. His soft, full mouth trembles like a ripple
in the surface of water. It is curious to see the paths of St. Francis
and Cimabue cross in this shadowy corner of the basilica. Cimabue painted a large number of frescoes in the upper and lower
church alike, virtually none of which survive. He was reputed to
be arrogant and perfectionistic, rejecting work that bore the slightest flaw in conception or technique. This was a new personality in
the thirteenth-century world, this temperamental individualist. In
those days a painter was a craftsman: the artist did not yet exist.
The craftsman did not throw away work because it was less than
perfect. He was the master of his materials, but he was not yet
their author.

Cimabue couldn't have cared less what his materials were
worth, that much is clear. He could see something beyond himself
and he made a path to it out of art. It was he who had to do it, for
only he knew where his vision lay. And it had to be right, flawless,
for what is the good of a path that doesn't lead where it is meant
to? In the painting of St. Francis, the saint says, "I am nothing";
the artist says, "I am everything." Cimabue reinvented painting by
reinventing the artist as visionary, as individualist, as risk-taker, as
criminal and hero. And he restored to the painted human form its
softness and mortality, its animal nature and the grandeur of its
emotion. This was the old knowledge of the classical world, which
the Christian story froze into a thousand-year hibernation. Now it
was to be reborn as something new. Humanity had insisted that a
link be forged between gods and mortals, but it was a long time before this new situation could be described: there were many rigid
Madonnas to be painted, many stiff and gilded Annunciations,
many primitive Nativities and stark Crucifixions before the con-
nection could be made. Now the artist-individual could paint the

St. Francis Preaching to Birds, by unknown artist

subject-individual, the creature who contains everything—good and evil, truth and illusion, life and death—within himself. Now, at last, he could begin to capture reality.

∾

There is a painting in the lower church by the unknown "Maestro di San Francesco" of St. Francis preaching to the birds. In its own way it is a masterpiece of characterization, according the Franciscan vision the full measure of its eccentricity. It is as tragicomic as its subject, for what could better illustrate the analgesic nature of insanity than the belief that one is understood by birds? Virginia Woolf, in her bouts of madness, experienced this delusion, and there is a photograph by Cartier-Bresson of the painter Matisse in old age, sitting in a room full of empty birdcages. White doves have roosted on top of their open prison: Matisse holds one in his hands. He appears to be addressing it, for like Francis he cleaved to what was innocent and childlike, to the positivism of dumb nature. "I have always tried to hide my own efforts," he wrote, "and wished my works to have the lightness and joyousness of a springtime which never lets anyone suspect the labours it has cost."

Francis preaches to the birds and the birds listen respectfully, lined up in neat rows on the grass. Their little heads are attentive: their eyes are bright. Like children they look up, for Francis is much taller than they. Their tiny beaks are lifted and their wings are folded at their sides. And Francis, in his cassock, speaks on, a tutelary finger raised, like a gentle lunatic in a public park. Upstairs there is a frescoed image of the moment he returned his clothes to his father in front of the bishop. It occurs to me that it is not for his godliness alone that the pilgrims come to worship Francis. His story, born as it is out of human psychology, is emblematic of the same consciousness that was simultaneously struggling to express itself in art. I am nothing; I am everything. Perhaps, after all, the pilgrims shush and glare at us for the same reason that we roll our eyes at them. It is the rise of the personal we are reverencing, in its different forms. It is meaning we have come for, of one sort or another. But most of all it is sympathy, sympathy that we want and must have, only sympathy, from bones or from paint.

∞

We go out into the gray, heavy afternoon. The basilica stands at the foot of the town, on a jutting peninsula of land where the earth falls away to all sides. Below it lies the plain, sinking into its own flat eternity like a separate element, so that from above there is the feeling of terminus, of the sea seen from the last cliffs that are the boundary of the habitable world. We walk away from it, up into the cobbled streets that twist and turn uphill. A small, hard

rain begins to fall, dashed down in handfuls. Every now and then
a monk passes by, impervious to the water. They wear immaculate
cassocks and sandals with belts of rope swinging at their waists;
they beam at everyone they see. They look like extras on a film set,
walking the antique streets beneath the artificial rain in their unblemished costumes. We have lunch in a restaurant, *gnocchi* made
by a chef who stands only a few feet away behind his little hatch
and beams at us too while we eat. The children want to buy a souvenir. We stand in a shop and look at nightlights made of molded
plastic, which show the Virgin encased in a plastic grotto that
lights up pink when it is switched on. There are T-shirts and table
mats and baseball caps, aprons and napkin rings and plastic pens,
figurines and Frisbees and extravagant embroidered wall hangings,
all bearing an image of St. Francis of Assisi. It is not Cimabue's
image: it is a computerized logo, a brand. There are expensive
porcelain statues, too, about ten inches high, that depict him
among the animals: birds have alighted on his hands, a deer rests
at his feet, a lamb lies across his shoulders. The statues are entirely
white: his monkish garment looks like a Grecian robe, falling in
long milk-white folds to his feet.

I myself had exactly this statue as a child. I was given it on the
occasion of my First Communion. It seems strange to me that they
should still be producing it, all this time later, so closely did I identify it with a phase of my own life. For years it stood on the mantelpiece of my bedroom, along with a blue china plaque bearing a
relief of the Virgin Mary in a wreath of china flowers. The plaque
is also for sale in the souvenir shop in Assisi. After I had left home
these things remained in my room in my parents' house, but then
several years ago my mother gave them back to me: I was grown
up, and had a house of my own to put them in. I didn't want them,
for I never felt that they were actually mine, and their presence in

this shop seems to prove it. There was something unsavory about them, something threatening: a sterility or morbidity, like the funerary displays in an undertaker's window. There they had stood on my childhood mantelpiece and though I never really looked at them their purity was dreadful and frightening to me, for it was clear that these were children's ornaments and when I glimpsed them out of the corner of my eye I saw children's graves. This was how the pill of religion was always forced down, with flavors too bitter and too sweet to mask one another. But I took the statue and the plaque back anyway, feeling that I should. When I opened the box again, all those years later, that flavor rose out in all its potency. I remembered how deeply the feeling of sterility had impressed itself on me, the feeling of Sunday, of nuns in their habits, of old bones, of disapproval and shame and of everything that could have no further issue, no continuance, in this world or the next. It all seemed to be paving the way not to heaven, nor even to hell, but to absolute and final nothingness.

Later still I found the statue again and put it in my children's bedroom. I don't know why I did: again, I only felt that I should. It looked anomalous and out of place, next to the little glass dolphin from Venice, the shell collection, the glass dome that you shook to make the snow whirl over the miniature Manhattan skyline. But one day I was in their room and I knocked it over by accident and broke it. I put the broken pieces in a shoebox, and hid them at the back of a cupboard.

A GAME OF TENNIS

It is late May and the days are hot now: the blue tent of the sky is stretched taut from horizon to horizon. The corn and maize have thrust themselves out of the earth, eager and unripe. They stand a foot high, stiff and fresh and green in their young sheaths. From the arthritic old wood of the vines that cover the hillside sprays of fringed, delicate, pale green leaves have burst out, and little hard reluctant clusters of tiny green grapes. In the garden there are flowers, not the soft, drowsy blooms of summer but gaudy, extroverted things on simple spearlike stalks that are the first to complete themselves in this race toward fruition, as though they were less innocent than the roses that still remain tightly packed into their pale buds: yellow irises with wagging yellow labia, vampish dark red gladioli, and a strange waxy cone-shaped flower of a volcanic orange color that stands erect on its thick, dark green stem. The bees drone ceaselessly among the purple cascades of wisteria. Sometimes snakes come out of the cornfield and ripple across the dirt track in the sun. Their emerald-green bodies swim through the dust, swift and silent. There are little scorpions too, with delicate pincers and tiny, probing tails. The geckos eat them, snatching them up and crunching through the crisp black shells with their narrow, reptilian jaws.

Jim drops by: he wants to know if we will play tennis. He says he can arrange doubles if we like. He has a friend in the vicinity who has a tennis court. He does not sit down: he perches on the wall of the terrace that faces the *castello* across the valley and smokes one cigarette after another, Marlboros whose glowing stubs he tosses into the grass. He has brought things for the children, tourist trinkets, *Madonna del Parto* key rings, posters of the Arezzo frescoes, a calendar with photographs of the local landscape. We look at the photographs: they ought to seem familiar but they do not. Some of them show views that we see every day, but there is something fake about them, something unreal. They are like copies, or forgeries: they seem to impose a stricture, a fetter, on what they have set out to represent. The Sansepolcro street in the picture can never be walked down; the photographic vineyard will never ripen and bear fruit. There is even a picture of our own *castello*, but it is not the same place from whose ramparts we looked down and saw the oblivious earth. It is imprisoned in its day, its hour, from which nothing now can liberate it. Jim doesn't want us to think he's spent any money on these things: before he got his taxi he used to run a bed-and-breakfast in the village, where he kept supplies of them for visitors. He's still got boxes of the stuff.

But the tennis: will we play? His friend, the one with the court, is keen to know. It is obvious that Jim himself is keen to know: he asks us how good we are, whether we play at home, and how often. Here at last is a subject capable of flushing Jim out of his habitual cover, out into the wide-open spaces of commitment. It seems that where tennis is concerned there is nothing compromised about him at all. He admits that he plays it: what's more, he says he's not bad. He's got an eye for a ball: he always did. When he was younger he played on the junior squad of a Scottish football team. He likes all games, board games too, Scrabble and Monopoly, though he isn't any good at chess. The world seems to interpose itself again when he speaks of chess. But he does like to knock a ball around. He always thought that that was what he would do with his life because it came so naturally to him. But there was a caesura, of what kind he does not say. He did not become a footballer. When he left school he went to Germany, to Bonn, and lived there for a while. His mother is German and she had family there. Then he went to London, and for ten years he ran a flower stall in Holborn. This was the period of his misbehavior, of his marriage and its subsequent failure, and of a whole host of dark occurrences of which he is not prepared to speak. It's no life, he says, running a flower stall. He made a pile of money, but it was hard and promiscuous work.

His friend with the tennis court is English. Her name is Amanda. She and her husband Roger own a hotel. He points to it with his cigarette from the terrace wall. Dimly I can see a stone façade lurking on a hillside behind a camouflage of trees.

Roger is another one of Jim's cronies. They play tennis together every morning. Roger, Jim says, is obsessed with tennis, though when he first came to the village he didn't know the first thing about it: it was Jim who taught him to play. It was worth his while teaching him, to get a regular tennis partner. Before that, the only people Jim could find to play with were tourists passing through for the week. Now Roger's quite good. And all he can think about is beating Jim. Every morning he faces him on the tennis court and is consumed by the desire to win. A devil takes hold of him: sometimes he gets so angry that he throws his racket around, and frequently he has stormed off the court. But the next day there he is again. He's taken a set off me once or twice, says Jim. He adds that this only occurs if he has spent the previous evening at the *castello* with Alfredo.

It isn't Roger, however, who wants to play doubles with us: it is
Amanda. Amanda's quite a good player, Jim says, and she's been
playing for far longer than Roger, but she hardly ever gets a game
because Roger won't play with her. It's a complicated situation,
Jim says, rubbing his eyes and throwing his cigarette into the grass.
But they're married people. Let them work it out.

∝

The children catch a gecko, and keep it in the chest of drawers in
their room for two days before I find out. I am angry with them. It
seems a cruel thing to do; the gecko has shed its tail in fright. They
cry and say they meant no harm, that they meant to tell me, but I
don't believe them. I sense that this was their secret. I have re-
tained my urban squeamishness about living creatures: they, on
the other hand, have become denizens of the garden and the
fields, intimates of the ants and snakes and scorpions. They see
few other children. The gecko, I feel sure, was kidnapped and
moved upstairs as a form of promotion: they wanted him for a
friend.

Tiziana tells them that if they catch a firefly, they will find a
coin beneath their pillows in the morning. One night we walk back
from the village as darkness is falling, and find the garden full of
white lights. Their motion is strange and beautiful: it is descriptive,
choral, a kind of silent music. The children dart through the darkness with cupped hands. The fireflies scatter in drifts, like embers.
Finally they catch one. For a moment it swims dreamily in the cave
of my daughter's fingers: she is lit up, electrified. Then it swims
away. She gets another, stealthy as a leopard. I watch her swift
body, knitted with the darkness. I watch her face in its enchantment. In our first week here I found her sobbing in her bed, missing her home and the girl she calls her best friend; and I was

smitten by guilt and a feeling of wrongdoing, a feeling that I
was not, myself, sufficiently adult to have imposed my destiny on
another. But she is my daughter: our destinies are better off in-
tertwined. And I see, in this moment, that she has become more
unified, more fully herself, that she will remember this time forever. It is a revelation by firefly-light, fragile and delicate, difficult
to grasp. She runs inside and is out again in a flash. She has found
a jar: in an instant she has caught a firefly and clamped down the
lid. It twirls inside, trailing a pale path of light. She puts it beside
her bed, but when I come up later I see that the light has gone out.
She is fast asleep. I put a coin beneath her pillow.

cx

The hotel is secretive, hiding in its deep screen of trees. There is
no sign or entrance, just two stone gateposts buried under ivy in a
glade of cedars. Beyond them lies a house, hidden lower down the
hill at the bottom of a steep track. It is evident that its owners have

no interest in attracting passing trade. Only from halfway down
the track can you see that there is a house there at all. It stands facing its own courtyard, while the valley falls away behind it. It is a
large, long, two-story building, very faded in color, delicate, with
white shutters and a colonnaded stone porch. The massive paneled wooden door stands open. The two rows of windows are dark
in the sun and the cavity of hall beyond the open door is dark too.

. There are people around, mostly men, lying on white plastic
loungers in the courtyard. Some of them are reading paperbacks
or magazines. Their sunglasses give their faces a blank, annihilating expression. Yet they seem quite harmless, lying there in their
baggy shorts and polo shirts and thick sandals. Most of them are
middle-aged, fleshy and white-skinned, with hair that is a little
threadbare on top. It is immediately obvious that they are not Italians: they are English. Only the English have those womanish,
fleshy bodies which wear their masculinity like an ill-fitting suit.
Nearby, a woman stands pushing a child on a swing. She is striking-
looking, tall and very slim, with long hair and a long gypsy skirt
and enormous gold hoops in her ears. She pushes the child back
and forth ecstatically, leaping on the upswing so that her skirt
swirls around her ankles. She tosses and strokes her own hair while
she waits for the swing to return, and then leaps again, trilling and
exclaiming, as though she were the child and the impassive creature in the swing were her toy.

Jim is wearing tennis whites, and carries a Fred Perry holdall
with two rackets inside. The hotel's clientele are a nice bunch, he
says, families mostly. Some of them come back year after year.
They pay a flat rate for the week that includes all their food and
drink. They socialize together, and eat their meals at a communal
table. Most of them never leave the precincts of the hotel.

Presently Amanda emerges from the dark interior. She moves slowly out into the light. She is wearing tracksuit bottoms and holds a tennis racket in her hand, but these accessories seem more symbolic than practical, like the objects that gods carry to represent their own attributes. Amanda could be a goddess of self-sacrifice, using the racket as a household implement. Immediately she is besieged from all sides, by women holding babies and men brandishing plastic beakers, by people with special dietary requirements and people with malfunctioning gadgets, by complaints and requests and urgent, intransigent needs, all of which she attends to, moving slowly through the crowd in her sunglasses, with her absent, goddess-like weariness, turning gently from side to side to scatter her wisdom upon the masses. The crowd moves along with her halfway across the courtyard and then they stop, like a herd that has reached a fence. She goes on alone, traversing the courtyard to where we stand waiting. A slender little dog with a narrow, sagacious face walks beside her. But even when she reaches us she doesn't halt: she merely gathers us into her train as she passes. Automatically we follow, a procession steadily making its way out of the courtyard and down a flight of stone steps, down amid lawns and trees, past children who call out greetings, past little arbors where men and women sit, past rockeries and shady benches, following the soft, slow form of Amanda, as though we were disciples who must follow our guru to the ends of the earth.

At the tennis court she finally stops. She removes her sunglasses. Her blue eyes have a sort of fractured, antique appearance, as though they had been broken into tiny pieces and carefully glued back together again. She lights a cigarette. She shakes our hands and ties the little dog by his lead. She passes her eye professionally over the children and questions them briefly.

Their answers appear to satisfy her: they are close in age to her own son. He will show them the treehouse, the rope swing, the sandpit. She will send someone to find him. He will be pleased to have the company of English children: most of the guests' children are babies. Paul has a nanny who keeps an eye on him. The children will be quite safe with her.

The tennis court lies exposed to the sun, on a shelf of land above the valley. We can see our house, the village on its mound, the far-off purple hills. The court, so big and bare, so open to the sky, reminds me of the sacred spaces of the ancient world, the vast raised altars of the Aztecs, the stone plinths of the Greeks. Amanda grinds her cigarette out on the asphalt. She is the goddess, the chief, come to the altar to accept her sacrifices, her offerings; and Jim is the priest who will eviscerate them and deliver them up. At first I am not cowed by Jim. He doesn't hit the ball particularly hard: he doesn't fly around the court, he doesn't grunt or smash or spin. He barely seems to move at all, and Amanda only bestirs herself when the ball is laid directly at her feet. Yet game after game falls to them: they rake them in unimpeded, like a croupier soundlessly raking in the chips across the smooth baize gaming board. It only takes fifteen minutes for them to win the first set. They are slow, easy, abstracted. We are red-faced and hot and heaving for breath. The sun chisels into the tops of our heads. Tongues of fire lick our bare skin. We strive and struggle but we are as powerless as those victims lashed to the altar in the glaring heat, from whom the satisfaction of supremacy must be exacted.

After a while I begin to discern Jim's method. He does not have strength or speed: what he has is an unerring eye. Never does he hit the ball out; never does he send it flailing into the net. No matter what he does, the ball invariably falls on the right side of the line. It is a kind of absolute, like a law of physics; and like a law of physics it bends the surface of reality into an arc of conformity with itself. A ball lands near Jim: with both hands on his racket he bats it high up into the air. We run around underneath it, looking up, trying to see where it has gone. Finally it comes rushing out of the sky like a meteorite and lands with a thud on the back line. One way or another we get it back. It lands near Jim again, because in all our struggle to find it and retrieve it a kind of reflexive politeness was left to determine the manner of its return. He bats it into the air a second time, higher, forty or fifty feet up, so that the ball is a black grain swimming in the distant fires of the sun. Our eyes are blinded: we run directionlessly, round and round like chickens in a farmyard. Eventually it thuds down in the outermost corner of the tramlines, and somehow, again, we get it back. We roam the back line, haunting our asphalt wilderness, rattled with expectation. Jim hits the ball with a spastic gesture, a movement almost private in its incoherence, like a grimace or a madman's twitch. From far down at the other end we watch its progress, rooted to the spot with disbelief. Slowly, stricken, the ball makes its way to the net, lumbering and low-flying, and when it has limped over it tumbles directly to earth and lies there amid the black mesh skirts.

Afterward Amanda is pleased. A light of satisfaction burns faintly in the distances of her pale blue eyes. Her face is smoothed out, as though some interior pain had been temporarily numbed. She offers us drinks on a terrace beneath a pergola. The little dog picks its way carefully after her over the grass and curls itself like a wisp of smoke at her feet. She tells us that she is forty, that she has run the hotel for more than a decade and brought up her three children here. Increasingly, in the holidays, they go to stay with relatives in England. They don't want to be here, with the constant comings and goings of guests. When they were younger they liked

it but now they find the motion sapping, the building up and dash-
ing down of temporary intimacies. But the hotel is very successful,
a success guaranteed by the xenophobia of the English, who flock
to this little principality with its values of the homeland: every
summer they are booked out from May to October. Amanda herself grew up in Italy, but she has grown disillusioned with it over
time. And now that the children too want to be elsewhere, she
wonders what the future holds.

One of the guests sits down at our table with her baby. She is
plain and perky, with a secretarial manner and spectacles on her
nose. She puts the baby in a high chair and ties a plastic bib around
its neck. Then she proceeds to feed it from a bowl with a plastic
spoon, addressing remarks sometimes to Amanda and sometimes
to the baby. Amanda replies in her gentle, abstracted manner. She
lights a cigarette and returns to our conversation, but the woman
taps her on the shoulder. Excuse me, the woman says, but I'd prefer it if you didn't smoke around the baby. Amanda apologizes and
instantly mashes her cigarette into the ashtray, where it continues
to smolder, its blue ribbon of smoke curling thoughtfully upward
through the vines of the pergola toward the early evening sky. The
woman casts her exasperated looks. Finally, with an expression of
distaste, she leans forward and takes the cigarette between the tips
of her fingers, and firmly extinguishes it herself.

℃

Jim calls. Amanda enjoyed her tennis. In fact, he hasn't seen her
enjoy something so much for years. She wants to play again, to see
us broiled once more in the sun and served up as victims at her
feet. To expedite her wish she has made us an offer: swimming for
the children in the hotel pool, and supper at the communal table.

When we arrive, a small boy is waiting alone in the courtyard. According to the children, this is Amanda's son. He has been standing there all afternoon, apparently, waiting for them to come. As soon as they arrive he tries to lead them away but they hesitate, a little shy. Their opposition confounds him: his white face is frozen, balked. He has been waiting for them to come, and now they are here, yet events are refusing to unfold. There is an obstruction, a blockage. It is not clear to him what the blockage is. He tries again to lead them away; again, they do not comply. His sturdy body stiffens. He has been objectified: in the face of their whims and desires he is as helpless and inflexible as a figure made of wood. Then, at last, they come, sprinting past him toward the tree swing while he runs gladly, heavily behind.

Today the courtyard is empty: it is very hot, a new kind of heat, white and dominating. Until now, people have sought the sun: today they seek the shade. There are no men with sunglasses and video cameras, no women with plastic feeding bowls, no tottering babies measuring out the parameters of their holiday with faltering steps. Where are they all? It seems they have been driven out of the open spaces, driven back by the white glare which has suddenly asserted itself, erasing the human dimension at a single stroke. In the distance we can see the swimming pool, just down the hill. It lies against the deserted green, a length of turquoise foaming with activity, like a strange human fish tank. There are so many people in it that I imagine them stacked in writhing layers all the way to the bottom. The whole community, it seems, has been displaced into this sky-colored rectangle. It teems with bodies, with inflatable rafts and rubber rings: a huge blow-up crocodile noses through the churning water. People dive in, or cannonball off the side, or haul themselves out slick and wet, like the first humans emerging from the primordial swamp. The sun bores indifferently into their wet, white backs. All around the fields lie motionless, stunned with heat.

This time Amanda is waiting for us on the tennis court. She stands at the perimeter fence, smoking and looking out at the valley. Her dog lies beside a bush, curled in its rim of shade. The court seems larger in the heat, as big and blasted as a prairie. We take our places and begin to play. For a while it is impossible to kindle a game on this featureless surface. We are too separate, too slow: there is nothing to get a purchase on. The ball is trivial and minute, coming out of the hot blankness. It is an effort, to move, to stir, to hit. Each stroke is like a reflex jerk to catch something that is falling. There is a momentary panic, a surge of adrenaline, then a slump while the ball buzzes away again. The sky pulses silently overhead. The sun presses, bears down, as though it would drive us into the earth. Amanda and Jim move indistinctly at the other end of the court. They seem tiny and remote. They win two games, but there is no succulence to their victory, no bite. We win a game, then they win another. There is a long, laboring game that goes back to deuce again and again. It is as though lassitude itself is winning. We probe blindly, like a thread probing at the eye of a needle, but the precision of success eludes us all. It is out of this formlessness, this lump of strategic clay, that the game suddenly begins to shape itself. The dull, hammering repetition of deuce begins to fashion something, a form, an entity. It attracts our notice: suddenly there is an object in our midst. We vie for possession of it, a little nonchalantly at first, for it is still featureless: it is a mere embryo, a seed. But its presence has a strange effect on Jim: he decides to leave two balls in a row for Amanda, and twice she sends them into the net. The fifth game is ours; the fight is on.

For more than an hour we play, while the hillside faintly rever-
berates with the cries and splashes from the swimming pool and
the sound of tractors passing in the valley below, dredging the
fields with dust. We are not conscious of these noises, though we
hear them; nor are we crippled by heat, for we have given ourselves over to it: we have passed through its white-hot refinery,
been purified, been smelted down and remade. Now we are as
lithe and liberated as the leaping figures on a Grecian urn. We are
as durable as clay idols fired in a kiln. Our adversaries confer, regroup, exchange wordless signs. The ball goes back and forth,
charged with esoteric significance. At last Amanda and Jim defeat
us, but there is sweat on their brows and a new hard light in their
eyes. Their victory has been less immediately satisfying to them,
but it has revealed a larger possibility of triumph, a greater conception of combat. Climbing the steps back up to the house, we
agree to play again the next day at the same time.

There is someone sitting at the table under the pergola: it is
Roger. He regards us with a satirical expression. When we are introduced he assumes a look of surprise that is more satirical still,
as though he had met us many times before and did not expect to
have to shake hands with us again now. The sun has set: the guests
are back in the courtyard. They wander through the blue light; they
hover and hang around, or gather in small murmuring groups, like
the survivors of something. They seem intensely aware of themselves as a species. Yet their purpose seems fragile, seems vague and
insubstantial, as they make their little circuits in the dusk, as though
looking for something to which they can attach the thread of life
and spin from it the web of an experience. From a distance their
little civilization appears doomed by a lack of conviction. Unoccu-
pied as they are, their power to superimpose intricacy on emptiness

is faintly unsettling. I can imagine them turning on one another, creating gods and victims, like the children in *The Lord of the Flies*. Amanda tells us of bizarre and comic incidents she has witnessed in her twelve years here, all of them so strange as to be scarcely believable: she herself, she says, can't believe that some of these things occurred, and yet they did. I attribute her tired, abstracted manner in part to these freakish tales, for it is hard to have faith in life when you have seen its credibility strained too often. Roger, however, does not like such stories: he wants to talk of successes, of high achievers who come back every year, of celebrity guests whom he numbers among his personal friends.

The children come. They have been swimming with Amanda's son and with his nanny, an Italian girl with long black hair and a melancholic face who strokes their heads distractedly with her painted fingernails. The boy sits on Amanda's lap. He looks contented and gnomelike, with his quizzical little face and round body. From the maternal throne he rattles away at his nanny in Italian. In English he is halting and tongue-tied, but his Italian self trills and chatters like a bird. He is like a creature in a fairy tale, a hybrid, a composition. In him the randomness of adult fortunes is distilled into permanence. Amanda repeats her invitation to partake of the communal supper. Absolutely, says Roger, after a finely judged hesitation. His face and neck are red and rigid: he looks as though he might suddenly, violently explode. Feel free, he says, waving his hand around to take in the hotel, the grounds, the whole enterprise. Just help yourselves.

Jim helps himself too. He is reticent: he eats little. I have the sense that he accepts the food not as a tax or perk, but as a favor, to whom I do not know.

ᖫ

For a week we play nearly every day. It is as though we have been waiting for our life in Italy to drift off its preordained course. We are tired of creating the world for ourselves. It seems we are ready to be diverted, to err, to be blown wherever the wind takes us.

The heat wave continues: we arrive with our rackets in the furnace of afternoon, and go silently out onto the court like gladiators striding out into the glare of the amphitheater. The hotel guests have returned to England, and another set have taken their place. We no longer notice them. It is the forms of our adversaries, of Jim and Amanda standing in the asphalt distances, that preoccupy us. Jim has been quiet on the subject of our new pastime. He turns up in his tennis whites, diffident and jocular. He never pleads a prior engagement, nor examines our commitment to this new course of events. His life is built on a basis of endlessly renewing transience, of people found and then lost, of habits easily formed and as easily broken. When the game is finished he waits for someone else to suggest another meeting, and he is pleased, acquiescent, when they do.

Within the matrix of the game itself, however, it is another matter. Jim is cunning, adversarial. As I am the weakest member of the group he constructs his path to victory through my side of the court. Every ball he hits, he hits to me. He harries me until it feels like a perverse form of attention. He does not trouble himself with gentlemanly thoughts of honor: for him, a point is not more decently scored because it has been won entirely through his own efforts. The easiest way to win a point is to encourage me to make a mistake, and so that is what he does. I quickly become enraged by this strategy. It is unclear to me why the rules of a game should be so distinct from the norms of social conduct. Why should tennis consider itself outside the obligation to be polite, to be fair? In life it is unethical to profit systematically from another person's disadvantage. But profit Jim does, and the more he does it the more enraged I become.

Then, after a while, I cease to care quite so much. I feel a delusion loosening its grip on me, the mistaken belief that a person is upright and good simply because he does not comport himself like a criminal. As Jim sends one ball after another into my domain I realize that people are by nature exploitative. It is merely that I have never been sufficiently the victim of their exploitation to know it. Now, it seems that I have a choice: to perish in the upholding of my own values, or to defend myself by any means possible. I am made to hit so many balls that the question is posed anew with unrelenting frequency. My ambivalence is exposed to a finer and finer degree, dissected and known to the last particle. Out of this flayed knowledge must I create something new; out of this final distinction between a ball that is returned and a ball that is not must the materials for survival be found.

It is unclear to me whether Jim factored in the possibility of improvement when he selected me as his victim. But I do improve: after all, I am hitting twice as many balls as anyone else, and many more than I have hit in my tennis career to date. I begin to evolve rapidly. I cease to be afraid when I hit. The ball comes flying toward me out of nothingness, and when I see it I increasingly feel the desire to impose myself on it, to create something, to manufacture some outcome. Its arrival no longer threatens me: it seems to come not out of a generalized fund of aggression but driven by needs of its own, the need to be shaped and directed, to be made articulate. It asks something of me, in its blind neediness. It wants to be possessed, turned around, sent out into the world again as my object. Jim begins to look a little surprised. All this time his eyes have watched me over the net, yellow and malevolent. Now I begin to see his face in profile, and once or twice even the back of his head as he runs to retrieve the ball from the back line. The invariable becomes the variable: he no longer always sends the ball to me. Once or twice he even winks when he places it at my feet after an absence.

We begin to win games, then sets. Once or twice Jim betrays annoyance when Amanda mishits the ball, and after that he leaves fewer to her, running to get them all himself. She doesn't mind: for her the sport, the situation, is all, and of course the victory that is laid at her feet at the end of it, like the victim's head laid at the feet of the watching empress. After that first time we don't accept her offer of supper at the hotel again, for we retain sufficient memory of ourselves to know that it is not fitting, not what we have come for, to wallow in the murky tank of Englishness, feeding and drifting with our own kind in their glass prison. But one night we all go out to a restaurant in the hills, a place far up a winding road that stands in a clearing among scrubby patches of commercial forest, where the raw stubs of trees stand in amputated rows in the pink earth, next to unfelled stretches whose turn it is evident will shortly come. The restaurant is next door to a shooting range. There are men down there in visors and earmuffs, firing rifles in the last light of evening. They shoot at targets, or at clay disks hurled mechanically into the air. The loud bangs and reports resonate around the tables on the deserted terrace. We sit down. Roger is there. There are some swings in the restaurant's garden and the children all gather there, playing in the indistinct light while the sound of guns rends the motionless air. Roger pours wine into everyone's glasses, all except Amanda's. Amanda does not drink alcohol. She is quiet, constrained, a little unhappy-looking. She has waited for her children to return and now they are here. She looks down to one side of her, like a Cimabue Madonna, as though she were silently corresponding with a sense of destitution, of a shortfall; as though it

is only in the presence of her whole family that she realizes something is missing.

The next day we beat Jim and Amanda at tennis for the first
time. Afterward Jim is curt and withdrawn. He says he isn't feeling
well today. He says he has a headache. He says he is going back to
his apartment to sleep it off. On the way home the children ask
whether we can do something else tomorrow. They don't want to
go to the hotel anymore. They want to go and look at paintings,
like we did before. They want us all to be together, joined by a
common interest, a common love.

I didn't realize that they had these feelings. It isn't only that the
paintings are a medium of togetherness and the tennis is not. There
is something else, some intrinsic value to art around which it becomes possible for the children to order their world. As for tennis,
it is a game, and games extinguish their own moment for good.
They are a way of killing time, and time, we now see, is our asset.
We mean to invest it wisely. We mean to make it last.

When next we see Jim he is his familiar self, darkly diplomatic.
He is glad we enjoyed the tennis, but he can see why we wanted to
give it a rest. There's not that much in it for the kids, he says, ruf-
fling their hair. And after all, he supposes we can play tennis at
home. He says this because he thinks that it is what we have con-
cluded ourselves. But I can see that he is disappointed.

However, he is worried that Roger offended us, that evening
up by the shooting range. We mustn't be offended by Roger.
Amanda would hate to think that we had been. He's just a bit ex-
cessive sometimes. He finds it hard to contain himself. Jim tells us
that when Roger and Amanda arrived here in Italy, Roger was
enormously fat. He was a massive mountain of flesh. He and
Amanda seemed happy enough. But almost as soon as they arrived, Roger began to lose weight. Jim didn't know why, but the

pounds just fell off him. It was quite dramatic, happening almost in front of your eyes. That was when he started wanting to play tennis with Jim. His fat man's frustration began to come out. The tennis made him lose weight even faster. And soon he was actually slim, for the first time in his life. The past didn't fit him anymore, like a fat man's gargantuan clothes.

Jim says he has to be going: he was on his way to pick up a fare and thought he'd just drop by to check up on us. He raises a hand behind him as he walks down to where his taxi waits on the drive and then he is gone, leaving us with images of giant trousers, of shirts like tents, of a fat man's jackets and jumpers, too big ever to be worn again.

GIANFRANCO'S STORE

In the drab gray folds of an English winter we speak of food. What will we eat in Italy? This is one of the details we consider, when we examine our voyage in its theoretical state. Human beings cannot proceed until their fear of hunger has been assuaged. We do not, of course, experience this fear: it is to celebrate its absence that we bring the subject up. There are countries you could go to where this is not the case. When I was a student, a girl I knew went to Russia for a term and came back grotesquely shrunken, with her clothes hanging round her in great vacant pleats. There had been nothing to eat, she said: nothing at all. Her teeth had turned black from lack of calcium. She had taken a two-day train journey in which the only thing she was offered was boiled chickens' feet.

From the distance of England the Italian cuisine seems to be all things to all people. It does not expect you to bend to its rigor, like the French. It is not rough and boisterous like the Spanish. It is soft and feminine and is adored in the highest circles, though it is not above a degree of prostitution too. But first and foremost it is kind to children. Consider the pizza: all around the world the pizza has come to represent the deepest forms of security known to the human palate. It is like a smiling face: it assuages the fear of complexity by showing everything on its surface. The pizza has nothing to hide, no dark interior, no subconscious fascination with its own viscera. That is why children like it. Indeed, it is the opposite of *haute cuisine*, which seems to be predicated entirely on the tendency of children to experience disgust. To eat lungs and livers and whole lengths of intestinal tubing is to declare yourself beyond revulsion and hence mature. As a child I was sent to stay with a French family, and watched in dismay as the mother opened a tin of chicken gizzards for lunch. No doubt I would have learned a valuable lesson in self-control if I'd eaten them. I'd have been as separate and contained as her own children were, instead of the lachrymose creature I remained, awash with emotion and homesickness.

Italian food has been widely taken up in modern times as a counterideology, to signal that such attitudes are in decline. Why should one be taught a lesson at suppertime? Why should one be made to grow up? And why should one be inducted at all into the darkness of our carnivorous nature? To bathe the palate early on in blood, to harden the body by the ingestion of other bodies: it was to extinguish sentimentality that such practices were inflicted, along with the strap and the cane. But sentimentality, like the pizza, is suddenly all the rage. Let the child's mouth be filled with comforting Italian starch, with substances that are soft and white and melting, with dough as pliant and soothing as his mother's breast. Let him remain forever babied by his beautiful mother cuisine, and never want to leave her. The English have latched onto the Italian breast with a vengeance. There are children in England who view the pizza as a talismanic icon, by which they can ward off the advance of any other foodstuff. There are children who eat pasta strictly unsauced and inviolate, like an ascetic religious order. And there are English adults who seek to intellectualize the *spa-*

ghetti alla carbonara in order to dignify their primal attachment to its farinaceous qualities.

All the same, there is a certain pretentiousness in the English conception of Italian food that I dislike the more for its infantilized origins. It seems unlikely to me, for example, that Italian magazines are quite so full of fetishistic images of their staple diet, of olive oil running in golden streams, of the red genital center of a sliced tomato, of pasta in its rigid and its flaccid state. After all, these things are not exotic: to the Italians they are as rudimentary as fish and chips. There is something a trifle pathetic in our English reverence for Parmesan cheese, our tittering fear of the aubergine, our belief that making fresh pasta is equivalent to building your own rocket and flying it to Mars. There is no particular need for us to be told again and again that cooking a risotto is as easy as standing on your head, but we want to hear it, and to hear it from the mouths not of Italian chefs but of native experts who understand that for the English the risotto itself is neither here nor there: it is merely the occasion, the transitional object that will facilitate our regression into infancy. We don't actually need to make the risotto to be healed by the philosophy that underpins it. It is merely the vehicle by which our childhood fears about food can be expressed. There are reasons why the English cookery expert does not approach us with the recipe for jugged hare (main ingredient: four tablespoons of blood): such things would only upset us. But in the innocent, sensory world of Italian food we can safely recall our primitive feelings of confusion and disgust for things outwith the body. The English cookery expert is the therapist who coaxes us through these labyrinths and rewards us with a spoonful of pappy rice, whether real or imaginary. He understands the repression of the English, a race reared for too long on kidneys and tongue. He understands our need to hear of the farinaceous south, where food is as milk from the mother's breast.

I, too, anticipate the Italian diet with feelings of relief, for I am not the omnivore I would like to be. There are whole continents I could never visit, so frightened am I by what I might be expected to eat. Even in France I exist in a state of constant suspicion and anxiety, rifling through my plate for signs of frogs or snails or songbirds, placed beyond the reach of self-consciousness or shame in my resolution to ask for everything *bien cuit*. A friend of mine describes how in a street market in China at night he bought something that was revealed by a streetlamp to be the jaw of a dog, but only after he'd eaten half of it. To China I will never go, nor to the territories of the Silk Road, where the travel writer Colin Thubron describes the horror of eating and drinking in near-total darkness, only to be told afterward what it is you have ingested. I will never go where they eat monkey brains or cats or guinea pigs, and though I love the literature of the past I would never go there either, to an England where larks and blackbirds lay beneath the pie crusts and something called headcheese was widely consumed. The English used to roast crows and eat them, and the idea of this funereal repast is worst of all. I am not proud of my revulsion. It is, I know, a form of stupidity. I do not wish to associate myself with the thoughtlessness of the modern palate, with its preference for deracinated flesh, for hamburgers and hot dogs and chickens crammed in cages. Better to eat a proud crow, with the sheen of life on its black feathers.

The Italian diet proceeds on the basis that isolation is the natural condition of a foodstuff. This is why it is so psychologically relieving. Nothing is hidden behind anything else. The tomato is one entity; the olive is another. The potato stands alone, and solitary is the asparagus in its sheaf of clones. To introduce one foodstuff to another represents a whole level of culinary attainment: it is a kind of marriage, inviolable, and hence requiring the utmost care to arrange. To form a group of three is an achievement even more significant. Often the third member of the group will be an herb, whose purpose is to enhance the attraction of the two principals. Sometimes the marriage will be so successful that the two food families will form a lasting alliance. A whole dynasty can spring from their union: tomato and mozzarella cheese, for example, together control an entire region of the national cuisine. It follows that to combine a large number of foodstuffs in a single dish would be tantamount to revolution. But every society needs its revolution, and Italy is no exception. That revolution occurred: its result was *ragù*. And *ragù* has given the Italian diet its manpower, its successful exports like *spaghetti alla bolognese*, the famous feat of engineering that is the *lasagne*.

But in food, as elsewhere in Italian life, the protection of interests is all. The introduction of new ingredients does not occur. The country's portals are firmly closed to the spices of the East, to the hybrid notions of the Pacific Rim, to the *satay* and the *flambé* and the *jambalaya*. Everything that is eaten in Italy is grown in Italy. And within those boundaries there are no outcasts, no unwanted elements. The old bread has a soup specially designed for it, the leftover risotto becomes rice cakes, even the hag-ridden cold spaghetti can find a home. These codes of alimentary conduct are deeply ingrained. There is only one way to do it and that is the way Mamma did, or better still Nonna, who after all taught Mamma everything she knew.

Tiziana's mother is a good cook. Every now and again she makes a rabbit stew for Jim, to shore up his commitment to the wooden hut. Rabbit stew is Jim's particular favorite. He is always

calm and conciliated after he has eaten it, as though someone had
injected him with a powerful tranquilizer. He doesn't cook much
himself. He'll make a fry-up, or sometimes mince and tatties. He
invites his English friends round for mince and tatties and ardently
believes that they enjoy them as much as he does. When he goes
home to Scotland he stocks up with tins of baked beans to bring
back to Italy.

I ask Tiziana what the local specialities are and she shrugs.
Ragù, she says, tossing her mane around proudly. I have noticed
that the restaurants around the village all have precisely the same
menus. What is the reason for this? Tiziana shrugs again. If I want
something different, she says, I should go to Anghiari. They have
different food there. Anghiari is a village eight kilometers away.
One day we do go there, and what Tiziana says is true. We are
given a kind of hot vegetable terrine called *sformata*, and a thick
tomato soup we have not encountered before. Tiziana nods when
we tell her. She knows about *sformata*. But nobody makes it here.

In our village there is a shop, known as Gianfranco's. It is a
small supermarket whose giant white-haired proprietor roams the
aisles in a stained white factory coat, bellowing and gesticulating
with his spadelike hands. He is like a polar bear with bespattered
fur, roaming its enclosure at the zoo. His enormous body is a kind
of spectacle, half bathetic, for he is old and unfree: he doesn't sit
in the shade of the café terrace like the other old men, so neat and
combed and compact, nursing their tiny glasses of dark wine. Instead he paces the stacked aisles with his loping gait, or shuffles behind the refrigerated cabinets, dipping his giant hand into salvers
of ground meat, paring red mottled disks from a length of salami
that fall one after another from the spinning circular blade onto a
sheaf of white waxed paper he holds in his palm. With the old
women he has a tutelary air as he provisions them for the day

ahead. With the young ones he is cheerful and avuncular. But the whole enterprise depends for its survival on the dominance of his personality, and so it is in the work of servicing his own myth that Gianfranco is the most assiduous. He laughs his giant, husky laugh; he bellows and roars, he sees things out of the corner of his eye that launch him into quixotic displays of chivalry. He pats the children on their heads and pinches the babies' cheeks. At the back of his shop there is a little bar, where certain customers are invited with great ceremony to partake of an *espresso* or a glass of Gianfranco's own wine, a profound, inky substance that drenches the blood with its indelible tannins. During these interludes Gianfranco's wife and daughter command the meat cabinet and the till: Gianfranco's surgeries at the bar are not to be interrupted. For ten minutes or more he is locked in deep consultation, like a minister with his aides. He leans over to rest his massive forearms on the dented chrome surface. The stained white coat presents its forbidding rear aspect to the shop. It is clear that interests are at stake. Advantages are being pursued, connections soldered. Customers are being reinforced in their commitment to Gianfranco's, which is smaller and more expensive than the supermarkets a few kilometers away in Sansepolcro. One day we ourselves are summoned to the political engine room and offered coffee and wine. Afterward we tell Jim, and he shakes his head. You must have been spending a pile of money, he says, laughing. Gianfranco must be banking on you paying for his summer holidays. He gives us directions to the Pam in the industrial park outside Sansepolcro.

It is in Gianfranco's that we study the lexicon of Italian food. The more we consider it, the more bewildering the absence of complexity becomes. We cannot translate our appetites into this abbreviated tongue. We cannot create something from ingredients like a child's building blocks, sturdy and unfaceted, primary-colored. Up and down Gianfranco's aisles we walk in our stunted condition, searching for food. There is cheese. It is white. There is young cheese and middle-aged cheese and old cheese. The young cheese is soft. The old cheese is hard. There is meat. It is red. There are olives like beads on an abacus. There is bread as tough and plain as a shoe. There is oil that revives the dead things, like an infusion of pure oxygen, or like an explanation for something unknown. There is pasta, blank as an empty page. We gaze at these things, tongue-tied and inarticulate. Our mouths are full of whole sentences that strain to be uttered and yet can't be. What is it that we wish to say? What is it that we want? The first generation of people who came to England from the Indian subcontinent bought tinned baked beans in English supermarkets which they washed of their sauce in order to be able to cook their own dishes. I can imagine the blankness out of which their whole conception of food had to be redescribed, the same blankness that I feel when I try to express myself in Italian and cannot find the words to do it. Sometimes I find a word that is similar to the one I wanted and I use that instead. But it was not our intention to translate our English diet: we planned to abandon it outright. We are not scouring Gianfranco's for the means of making steak and kidney pie. It is Italian food we want to cook, but it seems that we must have more than Italian ingredients with which to do it.

Jim renews his offer of mince and tatties. Imperiously, I refuse. I say that I do not want mince and tatties. I do not want the fodder of the cold North. Even the idea of them sticks in my throat. I want to remain loyal to the ardent suppositions of my own imagination, to my southern ideal, whether or not it exists. Jim is very offended. I have to apologize several times before he is appeased.

∾

In the field near our house there is a grove of olive trees. Their biblical forms are so ancient, their fruit so bitter: they are like the ancestors of the cultivated earth, so dry and bitter-tasting in their wisdom. Their subtle leaves make an antique filigree pattern against the duck-egg-blue sky.

The corn is starting to show in its pregnant husks and the fields sway with wheat. There are apricots and peaches and cherries at the fruit stalls. On the road to Arezzo people are selling truffles

and walnuts and mushrooms from the front doors of their farm-houses. We buy a bag of cherries and eat them, meditatively spitting out the stones. We buy big rough disks of bread. We buy a lettuce, and a fennel bulb like a swollen green knuckle. We buy a jar of truffle paste. The Italians make *bruschetta* with truffle paste. It is dark gray and closely textured. For a while we eat it, until I realize it is beginning to arouse feelings of disgust in my suspicious palate. The truffle paste makes me think of something horrible. One day, while eating it, it occurs to me that it is like eating puréed mouse.

We eat things that are red, white, and green, like the Italian flag. Yellow, that area of the food spectrum so favored by the English, has disappeared. So has brown, the color of sausages and gravy and a cup of tea. We eat hard little *cantucci* biscuits and drink *espresso*. We eat sheep's milk cheese and tomatoes. We eat the rough white bread. It is strange to eat the same things over and over again. It is a discipline in its way. It is not that we dislike this new, narrow range of satisfactions: on the contrary, the idea of eating at a wider scope begins to seem more and more grotesque. How could we ever have eaten curry one night and enchiladas the next? How could we have eaten chilies and chocolate bars and pancakes and wonton in the same twenty-four hours? Our promiscuity amazes us; our bodies remember by its absence the feeling of being thronged, of moving between hemispheres and time zones in the pause between breakfast and lunch, of being overrun, a hub of transient sensations like an airport terminal. It all seems now to have added up to a gluttonous neutrality, this specifying hunger that must select its object from the whole world. The discipline of our new regime is that of dissociating hunger from choice. Now there is only hunger, with sheep's milk cheese and tomatoes to satisfy it. It is important to be satisfied by what is known to you. Is that not a basic truth, biblical like the olive tree? But what of the desire to experiment, to roam, to know the whole of life in your allotted portion of it?

The Italians have an answer for that. It is *gelato*. In *gelato* the writ of choice runs free. Facing the refrigerated counter of the *gelateria* you are harried by choice, vexed and tormented by the power to select until you nearly beg for it to be taken from your hands. Everywhere I see people eating ice creams, children and old women, stringy teenagers and burly men in business suits, beautiful *donne* strolling down the smart Arezzo streets at four o'clock licking cones laden with *nocciole*. The oral neurosis of the Italians appears to deposit the whole of its weight in this realm of frozen childhood pleasure. Once, in a *gelateria* in the middle of Rome, I saw a man rush in from the street, where his limousine remained parked on a double yellow line, and order the biggest ice cream I have ever seen. He laid his leather briefcase on the counter and carefully spread a paper napkin over the front of his double-breasted suit. Then he applied himself with an extraordinary, determined rapacity to the heaped-up mountain, diminishing it with great bites like a giant and looking at his watch after each one, while his chauffeur sat outside and stared through the windscreen. This was an entirely private transaction, it was clear. I remember noticing that the outermost peaks and ridges of the ice cream remained erect and frozen around the bitten-out voids, so quickly did the whole thing occur. Usually it is not possible to eat an ice cream quite so destructively. The mound begins to thaw and lose its definition: it becomes transitive, passing from object to subject, until it wears the marks of irreversible ownership and gives itself up entirely to the passion of the human mouth. Sometimes the children mismanage this transaction. They work away at one side of the ice cream while the other languishes, collapsing into landslides and milky rivers that run across their clutching fingers. Or they dislodge the whole ball with the first contact of their tongues, and it falls to the pavement with an abortive *splat*.

The display at the *gelateria* is an artist's palette that awakens deep urges and anxieties, for it asks that something be created without hinting at the form it might take. Each color has its own significance, but it is sufficient unto itself. What human mood is ever so monochromatic, so pure? And how can one choose without transgressing the truth of one's own fundamental ambivalence? I notice that the children do not suffer from this difficulty. They are monotheistic: they choose the same thing over and over again. But the adults experience a distinct anxiety at the *gelateria*, which is the fear of misrepresenting their own desires. There are some people who regard this inexactitude in a detached way: they are slow to blame themselves for choosing what did not suit them. They are interested in what they have chosen, up to a point, but if the *pistacchio* is less delicious than the *cioccolata* they had yesterday, then that is the fault of the *pistacchio*. It is nothing to do with them. But there are others who take these things more personally. They must choose the right thing: they strain after the prestige of premeditated satisfaction. Some people are more easily made unhappy than others, that much is clear. Often I do not eat a *gelato*. I sit at a table while the others choose, and think about something else.

There is coconut and hazelnut and pistachio. There is grapefruit, lemon, lime, and mint. There is strawberry and raspberry and blackberry. There is *bacio*, kiss-flavor, an ice cream made of the Italian foil-wrapped chocolates whose infinite availability is a point of national pride. There is *straticella*, a streaky white-inflected substance that causes me to feel a strange constriction of the lungs.

There is nougat. There is *zuppa inglese*, a flavor so surreal that it seems to belong in a *gelateria* of the subconscious, a place where the artist's palette has given rise to whole sense memories and the ice creams have names like "Summertime" or "My First Day at School." *Zuppa inglese* translates as "English Soup." Apparently it is based on the recipe for sherry trifle.

One day we have lunch with Jim and Tiziana. It is Friday, and the restaurant in the village has fresh clams. Every Friday they serve *spaghetti alle vongole* and crowds of people come. The car park is full of lorries. The drivers sit alone, each at his own table. They are young men, clean-looking and disciplined. They gather like novitiates for the sacrament. I have seen these same types of men pull to the side of the road near Arezzo, where wan-looking girls in scanty clothes wait, hugging themselves with their arms. I have seen the cab door open and the girls clamber up, showing their underwear and their bare bruised legs, their spike-heeled shoes. The lorry drivers sit at their tables, clean and correct, while the waitress brings the dishes. She too is correct, reverent, as silent as an acolyte. She wears her shining hair in a plait down her back.

Tiziana has been learning English. She has just returned from her class in Città di Castello, where she goes twice a week as a form of obeisance to Jim. She does not perform this romantic duty with good grace. She resents it: it gnaws at her pride, to be reduced to reticence, for she does not find the English tongue congenial. It is not she, Tiziana, who is at fault: after all, her Spanish is fluent and her French is not bad. No, it is the language of the English that is to blame. It is an ugly language, indelicate, stodgy, filling the mouth with its cloying, indigestible sounds. *Th-th-th*, she says, grimacing as if she were being strangled. That *th* is enough to choke you. She is surprised the English don't choke on their own tongues. Jim begins to speak to us in English and Tiziana folds her arms and puts her nose in the air. *Blah blah blah*, she says loudly, after a while. *Blah blah blah blah blah*. *Th-th-th-th*.

The food comes. Tiziana eats little of hers. She cannot eat. Her mouth is still full of that English stodge. Jim remonstrates with her. It's a waste to leave so much food. She should have ordered half a portion. Now he'll have to pay for a whole plate of wasted food. Tiziana looks at him with narrowed eyes. *Scoteesh*, she says disgustedly.

I try to console Tiziana with my Italian. I say that I too feel humbled, feel childlike and impotent. It is hard to feel so primitive, so stupid. At this Tiziana looks exultant. Yes, she says, Italian is very sophisticated. It is the most sophisticated language in the world. It is very complicated and beautiful. English is not complicated. That is why it is difficult for an Italian to express herself in English. An English person could never learn all the words there are in Italian. Look at Jim, she says. He has lived here for twelve years and his Italian is *una merda*. But the English expect everyone to use their language. They will never understand the intricate mysteries of other tongues. They will never surrender themselves to the beauty of what is foreign to them. Instead they have to make an empire. Instead we all have to choke on English stodge.

The *spaghetti alle vongole* is so delicious that it has a kind of holiness about it. Trained as we now are on sheep's milk cheese and white Italian flour, purged of our promiscuous tastes, we are capable of understanding it. It is our prize, our reward, this understanding. A pile of empty clamshells remains on my plate like the integuments of a poem whose meaning I have finally teased out. Afterward Jim says he's going home to watch the French Open. Tiziana will not come with him. She declares her intention of going to look up an old friend in Sansepolcro. She is petulant and overwrought. In the car park Jim says goodbye to her. He is grim around the mouth. But a few days later we meet them in Gianfranco's and they seem excited, almost delirious. Tiziana is dolled up in a tiny skirt and high-heeled shoes. She flashes her eyes exultingly as Jim drags her up and down the aisles by her hand. Jim has a kind of charged resignation about him. They are buying steaks. Gianfranco has fantastic steaks, Jim says, with his best Dundee certitude. They're top-quality steaks, he repeats, so hang the expense. *Not Scoteesh*, says Tiziana, winking her fronded eye. She giggles as Jim drags her away again by the hand. We continue our slow progress along the aisles, patiently piecing together our diet as we piece together our Italian sentences, while Gianfranco waits behind his counter to pat the children on their heads and ask us how we are enjoying our long *vacanza*.

THE VEILED LADY

Vasari has the following to say about Raphael Sanzio, born in Urbino in 1483:

> With wonderful indulgence and generosity heaven some-
> times showers upon a single person from its rich and inex-
> haustible treasures all the favours and precious gifts that
> are usually shared, over the years, among a great many
> people. This was clearly the case with Raphael Sanzio of
> Urbino . . . Nature sent Raphael into the world after it
> had been vanquished by the art of Michelangelo and was
> ready, through Raphael, to be vanquished by character as
> well. Indeed, until Raphael most artists had in their tem-
> perament a touch of uncouthness and even madness that
> made them outlandish and eccentric; the dark shadows of
> vice were often more evident in their lives than the shining
> light of the virtues that can make men immortal.

Raphael was the only child of a painter, Giovanni Santi, a man
whose own rough upbringing had both lamed his talents and refined his humanity. Perhaps this is what Vasari means when he describes the meting out of heaven's gifts. Must the need to live and
the need to create be fed from the same allotted share? Thus the

artist is uncouth, or mad; and the man who chooses to be good will rarely have enough left over to fund his visions, unless he had the luck to enter this world undamaged. This was Raphael's position. Vasari notes that Giovanni refused to send his baby son out to be wet-nursed. Instead Raphael spent his infancy and childhood at home, with his parents. Giovanni taught him how to paint, and when he had ascertained the extent of his son's talents he set out to find a great artist to whom he could apprentice him.

The preeminent painter of that period was reputed to be Perugino, and so it was to Perugia that Giovanni took himself, to cultivate the friendship of the man whose powerful brand of parochialism is so aptly expressed in the name by which he became known. Perugino was an egotist-innovator of the Cimabue type; and just as Cimabue's fame was eclipsed by that of his pupil, Giotto, so Perugino's art was fated to become a pleasant suburb of Raphael's. Shortly after brokering the apprenticeship of his eleven-year-old son, Giovanni died. Raphael left Urbino and the world of his childhood, and went to Perugia to embark on a second childhood with a second father, whose self-portrait in Perugia's chamber of commerce bears the legend: *Behold Perugino, the greatest painter Italy has ever known.*

The sweetness of Raphael's disposition is often mentioned by art critics. It is offered as the explanation for many things: his popularity with influential patrons, his humility, the timbre of the paintings themselves, with their devotional secularism, their innocent-seeming love. Vasari, with his trademark enthusiasm, believed that Raphael's gifts of "the finest qualities of mind accompanied by grace, industry, looks, modesty and excellence of character" raised him above the sphere of men and into that of "mortal gods . . . who leave on earth an honoured name in the annals of fame [and] may also hope to enjoy in heaven a just reward for their work and talent."

It is a little curious, this feting of the virtuous artist. Like Mozart's, Raphael's art resolves itself in the childlike love of life: this is the harmonic home from which the world is investigated and to which the art is always striving to return. There are no scars in Raphael's art. There is none of the phallic aggression of Michelangelo, the worldliness of Titian, the tragic knowledge of Tintoretto. In short, there is no dimension of experience: everything is seen as if for the first time, is lived before our eyes, and sweetly remarked on. How relieving, to arrive at art by the route of pure sensibility! How pleasant, to look at Raphael's fond Madonnas and playful Christs and see only happy recollection there, not doomed foreknowledge!

When Raphael went to live with Perugino, his work consisted of filling in parts of Perugino's large frescoes on the master's behalf. Raphael was adept at this: indeed, he soon became better at painting Peruginos than Perugino himself. Raphael made copies of his master's work that could not be told apart from the originals. And, as Vasari puts it, "it was also impossible to distinguish clearly between Raphael's own original works and Perugino's." Raphael, it seems, was a little *too* sweet-natured. Where was his artist's ego, his vanity? Was he so well brought-up, so couth, that he broke his own chip of genius in two and shared it? One day Perugino went off to Florence on business and Raphael went to visit Città di Castello with some friends. While he was there he did one or two paintings in local churches, in his Perugino style. They would certainly have been mistaken for the real thing had he not signed them himself: as it was, the imitations brought Raphael immediate fame. He was invited to Siena to do some decorations in the library, and while he was there he heard a group of painters discussing the current rivalry between Leonardo da Vinci and Michelangelo, and the great works with which they were attempting to outdo one another in Florence. Raphael immediately stopped what he was doing and went to Florence. The sight of Leonardo's and Michelangelo's paintings woke him from his religion of Perugino. Yet how would this awakening express itself? Would he merely subsume himself in one artist after another? And their paintings were so anatomical, so mortal, so charged with emotion: how could Raphael, the obedient child, the ventriloquist, compete with these phallic male giants?

He returned to Perugia, where in the monastery of San Severino he painted a fresco and signed it, as Vasari says, in "big, very legible letters." Then he went back to Florence and in the space of three years painted a large quantity of Madonnas and other works for Florentine patrons. He painted the *Madonna of the Meadows* and the *Madonna of the Goldfinch.* He painted a portrait of Angelo Doni, a wealthy Florentine wool merchant, and of Angelo's wife Maddalena, in the style of Leonardo's *Mona Lisa.* Yet in spite of his popularity and his ceaseless flow of commissions, his artistic "awakening" and his newly declamatory signature, his good looks and his amiable personality, Raphael remained locked out of the reality his contemporaries were charting like a newly discovered continent. What were they seeing? What did they know? And how could he come to know it too? For Raphael's Madonnas were just sweet, beautiful recollections of childhood, and his portrait of Maddalena, though he worked and worked on her hands and her clothing to make her human, lacked what is more human still, what is invisible to the naked eye. It lacked the very thing that makes the *Mona Lisa* seem to smile: mystery.

α

The train to Florence passes through tunnel after tunnel, long interludes of darkness that suddenly give way to bright, bleached passages of intricate daylight, just as dark tunnels of sleep seem to snake their way toward dreams, bursting into color and detail and then plunging back into a swift-running obscurity. The hot, dusty vineyards of Chianti flash past; here and there a house stands remotely in the hills. Then we are in a tunnel again, traveling without seeming to move, thundering at a black standstill with a clamor that might break open time itself. And indeed the time machine of popular imagination never actually stirs. It merely gathers in intensity, as though an effort of will is all that is required to enter the past. I don't suppose this idea has anything to do with looking at paintings, but the procedure is the same. It is a matter of intensity, of will. It is possible to look at a painting and not see anything at all. There must be an offering of the self before the painting will open. There must be intensity, or the past will stay locked.

Florence station is slightly seedy, with the scummy froth of litter and souvenir stalls and fast-food places that is the residue left by tourist tides that sweep ceaselessly across its reef of treasures. In the city there are people everywhere: they form great winding queues, like roads whose destination lies out of sight. Several times I see people automatically joining them, apparently without knowing where they will lead. There are Japanese and German and French, Spanish and Dutch and American. They drift around the city in concertinaing herds, their guide at the front like a shepherd. The guides hold sticks raised in the air. Each one has a flag or a brightly colored ribbon tied at the top. Their flock wears the same ribbon, so as to be identifiable in the crowds. There is a group with yellow ribbons tied around their throats. There is a group with tartan caps. It is like a strange medieval pageant or festival. They flow and counterflow in the variegated spaces, each one drifting out and contracting like a single, liquid creature. They bunch up in alleyways and fan out over the piazzas; they wind like serpents along the crowded pavements. They congregate at Ghiberti's *Gates of Paradise* and the guides shout across one another in their different languages.

It is very hot in the city. The buildings stand in dusty chasms of shadow and light. The traffic crawls along the Via della Scala. The blue sky is far off and remote. The Piazza del Duomo is a crucible of glare, with its white marble tower and cathedral and baptistery. The crowds look half calcified in the bleaching light: in their individuation they seem to be helplessly disintegrating, breaking down into smaller and smaller units. We move along a congested alleyway toward the Piazza della Signoria, where a riot of café terraces and horse-drawn tourist carriages and pavement hawkers selling African jewelry is under way. People push and shove rudely, trying to get what they want: photographs, food, a tea towel bearing the cock and balls of Michelangelo's *David*. There are so many people that the sculptures on their plinths in the Loggia dei Lanzi seem truly to be the gods they represent, gazing down on the awful spectacle of mortality. I have seen a fifteenth-century painting of the Piazza della Signoria, where children play and the burghers of Florence stroll and chat in its gracious spaces, while the monk Savonarola is burned at the stake in the background outside the Palazzo Vecchio. Here and there peasants carry bundles of twigs, to put on the fire. Now our violence is diffuse, generalized: it has been broken down until it covers everything in a fine film, like dust.

The long, colonnaded façade of the Galleria degli Uffizi stands in a side street, between the piazza and the river Arno. It is

as shady and civilized as an arbor here, despite the queue that runs four or five people deep all down one side and up the other. The light from the water is soothing, mesmerizing, on the high-up windows. The people in the queue have an eternal look about them, for only a small number are admitted every hour. The gallery is visited by appointment: there is a separate door for people with tickets. A young man in a dark, immaculate suit stands there, bowing and ushering the ticket holders in without delay. The people in the queue look on from behind their ropes. They will be there forever. They are bound into a thick, hot cable of bodies that runs as far as the eye can see. There are people with children, people with large suitcases. Again and again, those with tickets arrive and are whisked into the cool interior before their eyes. We ourselves have tickets: we had to wait two weeks for our appointment. How sparse the world's treasures are! And how hungry, devouring hour after hour of life! It is almost as if they wish nothing more to be created.

Inside, the building is deep and tenebrous and hushed. We go up a great stone staircase, rising through layers of light, past fragments of Roman sarcophagi leaping with mythical creatures, past cracked marble torsos and far-seeing Hellenistic faces, up and up as though we were rising through time itself. At the top there are long galleries like avenues, filled with an unearthly, watery light. Far below the river can be seen, broad and fertile and opaque. It is like a strange kind of heaven up here, where sculpted gods and goddesses stand along the walls as though milling in the halls of eternity. They are so well guarded, so secure in their possession, so superior to the dusty streets below, teeming with life. I remember the people queuing downstairs, held like waters at a dam. What pent-up force waits there? What do they want? Why do they accept the authority of this heaven, and their banishment from it?

Yet it is true that all those people couldn't fit up here comfortably. I don't suppose we would worry about comfort if it were left up to us. The yearning for beauty has not surrendered entirely to the desire to be comfortable, that much is clear. An overgrown humanity trying to fit into the narrow, beautiful past, like a person in corpulent middle age trying to squeeze into a slender garment from their youth.

We pass through the rooms, past Cimabue and Giotto, past Simone Martini's Annunciation that seems spun from a cloud of gold. This is the old world, where man is unfolding as though from a bud, by increments. Simone's Madonna draws her cloak around her throat, while with her other hand she marks her place in her book with her thumb. Nearby, Lorenzetti's Christ child grips the Madonna's chin, his fingers at her mouth. Slowly, awareness comes. The figures begin to look out of the paintings, out into the world. Fantasy and reality succeed one another in waves, going forward and then back and then forward again, but always climbing, encroaching on some imperceptible common goal. The Madonnas change, the Christs change, the saints acquire different faces. Then there is Leonardo's Annunciation and the Madonna becomes Mary, a girl of flesh and blood. Perugino's Christ in the garden at Gethsemane is a good-looking young man with a fresh, sensitive face. In Mantegna's Circumcision two women stand talking in asides, slouching; one of them rests her arm on her own stomach, as women do when they aren't self-conscious, while her other hand abstractedly touches the hair of the little boy who stands beside her. Suddenly we are on the firm footing of life, though the subjects have barely altered. We have arrived at the grandeur of the human. By the time we reach Correggio's *Adoration of the Child*, Mary looks like what she is: a real woman who has put on a blue cloak in order to pose for the artist.

There is a self-portrait by Raphael in the Uffizi. It is a strange painting, of a frail, wistful-looking youth clad in black. It is faintly ascetic, even depressive: it is a portrait of Raphael's captive ego.

Self-Portrait, c. 1506 (tempera on wood), by Raphael (1483–1520)

Nearby hangs the *Madonna of the Goldfinch*. It was damaged in
the mid-sixteenth century, when the house of Lorenzo Nasi, who
owned it, was destroyed in a landslide. Carefully it was pieced back

Madonna of the Goldfinch, c. 1506 (oil on panel), by Raphael

together, but a long, sad scar runs through it, all the way down the Virgin's breast and belly and lap. Shortly after he painted the *Madonna of the Goldfinch*, Raphael's mother died. The woman in the painting is neither real nor divine: she is an emotion, a flesh-memory. The Christ child leans back against her knees, his small foot resting on her larger one, his head tilted back into her lap. The other child, St. John, is holding the goldfinch. He is showing the bird excitedly to the Christ child and the Christ child is reaching out halfheartedly to touch its head, gazing at his friend with sorrowful, almost baleful eyes. He won't stray one inch from his mother to touch the bird. He has wedged himself between her knees. It is John who holds the bird, and it is John the Virgin looks at from her downcast eyes. It is John on whose bare shoulder her fingers rest.

Michelangelo's *Tondo Doni* (*Holy Family with the Young Saint John*) hangs close to the *Madonna of the Goldfinch*. Michelangelo's attitude to the male competitor John is clear. He has put him in the background, behind a wall with the rest of lesser mankind; a respectful urchin in an animal skin who gazes up, lost in admiration for the hero of the hour, the vigorous Christ who is seen clambering naked from his father's lap over the form of his mother and clutching her hair for balance. Mary has her arms outstretched to receive him, but it is far from clear that she is his destination. He looks as though he means to climb out of the picture and head off into the world to collect his due. He balances on top of his parents, the absolute egotist, crushing them underfoot and flashing his virility as he goes. This was perhaps the first time the Christ child was depicted towering over the Madonna, a lithe lass with a husband too old and too cautious for her. This son already owns his mother. She reaches for him while Joseph hovers, gray-haired and anxious, but she cannot possess him. He has already escaped

his parents. He wears a band of victory in his hair, his only
adornment.

∽

In 1509 Raphael left Florence and went to Rome. A distant rela-
tion of his, Bramante of Urbino, was working for Pope Julius II
and had persuaded him to commission Raphael to decorate a se-
ries of rooms that had just been added to the papal apartments.
Raphael went straightaway, and when he arrived at the Vatican
found numerous artists at work there, including Michelangelo.
Raphael was given a lot of work to do, and for everything he did
he received the highest praise. But praise has its own limits. The
question of rivalry, which had dogged Raphael, though he had repressed it by a mixture of imitation and charm, now came to tor-
ment him face-to-face. Pope Julius admired Raphael, but it was
Michelangelo he loved, Michelangelo he fought with and ban-
ished and begged to come back, Michelangelo who rebelled and
was somehow loved the more for it. This passion of patron and
artist found its best expression in Pope Julius's desire for Michelangelo to sculpt his tomb. He had a drawbridge built between his
room and Michelangelo's, so that he could come and go as he
wanted, and inspect the progress of his memorial. Raphael had
never experienced this desperate, exacting kind of love. In art he
was the lover, the aspirant, not the beloved. He was the one who
hopèd to please. But was there something else, a serpent, a secret
desire to be first and best that masked itself in his humility? And
was it in fact this mask that formed the blockage in Raphael's
art, its stubborn separation from reality? There is jealousy in the
Madonna of the Goldfinch, but there is neediness too. Raphael needed
something: but what? Michelangelo went around having fistfights
and feuds with people, and dreamed of making giant statues in the

Carrera quarries to leave behind him, as the ancients had. All he seemed to need were blocks of marble big enough for his ambitions, and the freedom to carve them. How was Raphael to go about satisfying his own unacknowledged need for greatness?

While Michelangelo was out of Rome, Bramante and Raphael set about trying to undermine his reputation. They suggested to Julius that to build his own tomb was to invite his own death. When Michelangelo returned, he was told by Julius that work on the tomb was to be suspended. Instead, he was to paint the ceiling of the Sistine Chapel, a job at which Raphael and Bramante were confident he would fail, for Michelangelo was principally a sculptor, not a painter. Michelangelo locked himself into the Sistine Chapel: no one was allowed in, not even Julius. It seemed that to fetter Michelangelo was simply to make his myth the more powerful. Soon, all of Rome was fixated by the mystery of what lay behind that locked door. Then, according to Vasari, Michelangelo had to leave Rome for a few days, and while he was away Bramante got hold of the keys. He and Raphael went in to look. And what they saw, of course, was the preeminent artistic achievement of the Renaissance and perhaps of the whole history of art, past, present, and future.

Seeing the Sistine Chapel, Raphael experienced the overwhelming reaction of his primal reflex, imitation. He immediately went and repainted whole parts of his own work in the Stanza della Segnatura in the style of Michelangelo. After the cataclysm and shame of rivalry, he retreated behind the mask of humility, never to come out again. With the world's greatest painter as his template, he became a far better artist. And to the art critic's eye he had gained far more than he lost, for in the end his borrowing of such greatness amounted to greatness itself. Not everyone who sees a Michelangelo can go off and paint a Michelangelo. Raphael was almost as good at painting Michelangelos as Michelangelo himself. His captive sensibility needed a love object to express itself. It is in this, perhaps, that the critics perceive what appears to be Raphael's sweet disposition. They see it as humility, not the devious workings of a repressed ego. They see it as a tribute, not a theft. But Michelangelo saw it as a theft.

∞

Raphael died young, at thirty-seven. He was, Vasari says, "a very amorous man with a great fondness for women whom he was always anxious to serve." His passions were more powerful in the sexual transaction than in the artistic, for in sex there is reciprocity. The love is not praised: it is returned. This, it is clear, was a compelling experience for Raphael. Perhaps, like the Christ child in the *Madonna of the Goldfinch*, constant bodily contact with a woman, in other words his mother, was his way of seeing off the male competitor, who could not dislodge him physically even if he stole her attention in other ways. On one occasion, he was so besotted with a woman that he was unable to concentrate on the work he had undertaken painting the *loggia* of Agostino Chigi's Villa Farnesina until she was installed there with him.

When Raphael first went to Florence as a youth, in his Perugino years, it was Leonardo da Vinci who initially attracted his succubus-like notice. Leonardo's women were so beautiful: the inclination of their heads, their soft, sympathetic expressions, their golden atmosphere of smiling female mystery. Straightaway Raphael's Madonnas began to smile too, and incline their golden heads. The *Madonna del Granduca*, painted in 1505, emerges out of darkness like a figure in a dream, or like the love object emerging for the first time from her anonymity. She holds the Christ child upright against her side, and yet it is he who appears to be holding

Sistine Madonna, 1513 (oil on canvas), by Raphael

her. One hand rests proprietorially on her bosom, the other on her
neck. He looks out into the eyes of the world, displaying her and

owning her, this woman he has brought out of the shadows and whom he seems to grip lest she recede again. Later, when he was painting Agostino Chigi's *loggia* in Rome, Raphael was asked where on earth he had found his model for the nymph Galatea. She was so beautiful: how could she possibly exist? Raphael replied that she wasn't painted from a specific model. She came from an idea he had in his own mind. It was, of course, here in the Villa Farnesina that Raphael's mistress was now living with the purpose of oiling the wheels of his refractory genius. Did the presence of the real woman permit the ideal woman to be imagined? Or was this mistress, in fact, the living model of Galatea's wondrous beauty whom Raphael, the possessive child, denied and hid away from other men?

Raphael's friend Cardinal Bernardo Dovizi, who found the painter's promiscuous behavior disturbing, believed that marriage would be the answer to Raphael's problems. Here Raphael encountered a rare and insurmountable certainty in himself: he did not want to get married. Perhaps, after all, the ideal woman, the Madonna, could not be conflated with the sexualized woman, the courtesan or mistress. But it was in the function of Raphael's devious ego to give the appearance of being dominated and directed by other men: always, it was by this route that his true desires became known to him. In this case, however, the directive and the desire were mutually hostile. Typically, Raphael decided that what he wanted was not to get married but to be a cardinal, like his friend. Pope Julius was dead by now, and Pope Leo, a great patron of Raphael's, had in fact insinuated that Raphael might receive the "red hat" once he had finished the hall he was painting. But Cardinal Dovizi had meanwhile elicited Raphael's promise to marry his niece. Imitation and obedience collided: he couldn't be a cardinal *and* get married. And in the prospect of marriage

Raphael appeared to glimpse the frontier of his civilized self, beyond which lay the undiscovered hinterland of his true nature which he had never dared to enter. How can an artist attain greatness if he never knows the truth about himself? In the same way, I suppose, that a blind man can see the world, because people describe it to him. He refines his other senses. He learns to recognize the truth, even if he can't personally see it.

Raphael responded to his dilemma by pursuing his pleasures, as Vasari puts it, "with no sense of moderation." He contracted syphilis and became very ill, but because he concealed from the doctors the cause and nature of his illness they diagnosed him with heat stroke and proceeded to bleed him. From this last piece of self-deception, Raphael died, in 1520.

α

The *Sistine Madonna*, which Raphael painted in 1513, shows a rather different mother and son than the golden women and possessive boys of his earlier years. This mother is smaller, more lifelike, less dominating. The boy is larger and more confident. He is beautiful, with lustrous hair and a lithe, well-modeled body. He does not clutch or grip his mother. He reclines in her arms, one leg crossed at the knee, like a young man sitting easily in an armchair. He seems satisfied. Only his head, which rests unconsciously against her cheek, betrays the fact that she remains his object, his desire. For a moment he looks as if he might be getting up and going somewhere, but that resting head says it isn't so. He is more relaxed, that's all. The woman is more real to him. She isn't a golden ideal he fears will be stolen from him. He doesn't cling onto her. His hand lies lightly on his own leg. It is she who holds him, supports him, of her own volition.

In the Uffizi there is a late painting by Raphael, of Pope Leo

Portrait of Leo X (1475–1521), Cardinal Luigi de' Rossi,
and Giulio de Medici (1478–1534), 1518 (oil on panel), by Raphael

with two of his cardinals. Leo is a big, heavy, fleshy-faced man,
padded with garments of velvet and embroidery. He is powerful,
ugly in his power. His embroidered robe is more beautiful than he.

In his hand he holds a small magnifying glass, with which he has just been scrutinizing the great gilded book that lies on a table in front of him. Now he gazes forward, his brow faintly crinkled, his eyes calculating: clearly he is pondering some problem of state. Of the two cardinals attending him, one looks straight ahead, like the guards outside Buckingham Palace. The other looks out, askance, at us. He is in young middle age, a little unshaven, with dark eyes that are half innocent, half knowing. With both hands he grips the back of the papal chair, where Leo sits immersed in his trance of male authority. It is those clutching hands that suggest to me that this is a portrait of Raphael himself. And he has taken such care to describe the signs of age that are encroaching on those childlike eyes, the receding hairline, the lines around brow and mouth, the tired pouches that hang under the lower lids. With his steady gaze, this man is asking a question. Who am I?

Across the river, in the Pitti Palace, there is a portrait of a lady. It is by Raphael. Its title is *La Donna Velata*, "the veiled woman." Her veil is rather spectral: it has been pushed back from her face, but it seems that it might close around her again, like a shroud. How fine she is, though, in her moment of life! Later, in the *proprietario's* library, I read that this woman is believed also to have been the model for the *Sistine Madonna*. Here, she is permitted her own reality, her necklace of amber-colored stones, her lovely dress with its gold piping, her white undergarment with its delicate gathered neckline and little ribbons tied in bows. In her hair, just where the veil has been folded back, she wears a single pearl. Her hand rests on the stiff material of her dress where it covers her breasts. It seems to be a gesture of invitation, but it hints, too, at a feeling of separation from her own finery. This is the woman who holds her child so willingly, so generously, in the *Sistine Madonna*. I wonder whether the veil is, at last, the symbol of Raphael's self-knowledge.

The Veiled Woman, or *La Donna Velata*, c. 1516 (oil on canvas), by Raphael

It is he who veils her, for her body is the drama of his subconscious. The veil is the psychic rift which separates one image of her from another. Is she to wither in her casket of gold piping and amber-colored stones? Is she to remain alone, like the pearl in her hair? When she fingers her cloth-covered breast, what vision of love rises in her large, dark, heavy-lidded eyes?

We take the train back to Arezzo. It is late afternoon and the carriages are crowded. We sit with the children on our laps, and I listen to the conversation of four Englishwomen who are sitting across the aisle. Their own laps are full of purchases from Florence boutiques: they are returning to their rental villa in the hills. They are in their early sixties, I suppose, smartly dressed, with hair cut short and firmly styled. They seem to have outlived the world of men, of marriage and motherhood and children. They laugh hilariously at anything any one of them says. They are a third sex, these happy materialists. They have outlived it all, the mystery of men and women: it has passed, like the day's heat has passed and left behind its warm, tolerable aftermath of evening. The children have gone to sleep. I close my eyes and find that the *Donna Velata* is there. I think of the cold stones on the white skin of her throat. I think of the stiff gold piping of her dress, and of the single pearl, hanging in her hair like a droplet of ice.

VOLCANOS AND THIEVES

South: we are going south. It is time to pack up the house and say goodbye to the green valley and the *castello* and the *proprietario*'s library. It is time to forswear *ciaccia* and Gianfranco's store and the flowers in the garden whose little arc of life we have known so intimately. What is the significance of this knowledge? In the afternoon, the light falls in slanting golden panels through the windows of the silent rooms. The track winds blindly down the hill to the valley floor. The hills simplify themselves into primitive, mysterious forms as evening comes. The fields and woods and villages merge into their blue mounded distances. And in the morning their detail is born again, the fresh patchwork of hills and houses and trees, the close-textured countryside, the slender leaves with their dainty, tentative veins, the many-petaled flowers, the flossy white spiders' webs knitted among the roadside weeds, the armies of ants trickling in the dust, the blades and tresses of corn and wheat that separate and separate until they seem to disclose the last blond grain of infinity itself. I know the silken strands of the spider's web, and the muffled white form of the sac that hangs at its center. I know the froth that foams like spittle on the fibrous stalks of the weeds. I know the black bead of the gecko's eye and its darting tongue. What else is there to know?

One day I hear a sound like the sound of rushing water, coming from the side of the house. I go out to look, and see a swarm of bees standing in a great·black column on the path. They have escaped from a nearby honey farm. A man comes with a little wooden box to collect them. Inside the box there is a queen. The man sits in his car with his wife, eating sandwiches and waiting for the bees to go in. Then he drives away again, with the great black column folded into the little box, like a magician.

There is a farewell dinner at a restaurant not far away, and afterward, in the darkness of the car park, Jim puts a letter into my hand. It is a kind of love letter, except that the love is mostly too damaged to be recognizable. But in one place Jim says that he almost wishes we had never come to the village. It would have been easier for him. It would have been easier, he says, not to have known us, than to know us and us not be there. I am struck by this. I think about it often. Is knowledge by itself a form of pain? Is it redundant, when it is not underwritten by possession? We have possessed virtually nothing in our life in Italy. In England, I became increasingly sure that to possess something was to arrest your knowledge of it, because the thing

itself is no longer free. For me the pain of knowledge is a tonic, an antidote to the pall of possession. But there is an element of death in knowledge, and it is this, I suppose, that Jim dislikes. Knowledge is what remains to the human mind once the possession has been lost. It is the reliquary of the vanished object. Its presence is painful, because it signifies that what was known is no longer there.

∽

South: is it possible that, having come all this way down, we are to go still further? When the children swim, they sometimes throw coins into the water, and I watch as they dive to the floor of the pool to retrieve them. There is always a transition, when the momentum of the dive gives way to the resistance of the water, and they must swim to descend the last few feet to the bottom. I see the change in the movement of their bodies: there is a second of panic and then a kind of liberation, a struggling free from the world of the surface. Down they go, with no air left in their lungs, down into the underlying silence where there is nothing further to remind them of life. It is as though they are entering a place they know but had forgotten. I watch them reach out with green-white fingers, their hair suspended in the water like mermaids'. They are so unhurried, so free of need. They seem, briefly, immortal. Then their little hands close around the coins and they shoot straight upward, all urgency, as though fearful that their brief forgetting of the world above might have made it cease to exist.

We put our things in the car and we put the car in a garage in Arezzo and we board the noon train. We are to voyage among thieves and volcanos: we are traveling light. Outside, the world lies in a trance of heat. The temperature clock at the station reads thirty-eight degrees. The suburbs of Arezzo glide by, stunned in the dust. Then there is a brown vista of the pitiless plain, fringed by indifferent hills. The children are somewhat shocked to discover that we have left the house in the valley for good. They wish to know why we have done this. They loved that house: they were under the impression that as no one had said otherwise it had become, quietly, our permanent home. Though we have explained our plans to them many times, it is clear that for them an explanation remains an entirely theoretical experience. It offers not the slightest protection from their feelings, which hit them with the force of hammer blows. Now the feeling of loss is upon them: they look for some way of defending themselves. Did we sell the house? they ask suspiciously, as though we were known for doing this behind their backs. No, we explain, we never owned it. It belongs to someone else. They mull this over. They remember the house in England—they hadn't wanted to leave that either. It upsets them to remember that house, where they lived for three years. Their feelings about the house in Italy are really their feelings about the house in England in disguise. They realize that they had begun to forget it, and forgetting is the deepest loss of all. The real wound has been uncovered. They become tearful. Why did we leave the house in England? Why?

The hot, heartless world meanders past the windows: the train stupidly follows its monotonous southern impulse. There is a nun sitting quietly in the corner of our carriage. She is small and plump in her dove-gray habit. Her tiny feet are crossed neatly at the ankle beneath her long skirts. She has a broad, flat face and a high, rounded forehead like the forehead of an elderly china doll, with the close-fitting band of her veil at the top. She seems so distant from the experience of pain, so dry and plump and spotless, so indefatigably neutral, with her wooden crucifix as chunky as a child's toy: she sits like a mannequin in her corner, old and virginal, looking out of the window with small, pale blue eyes. What does she know of loss? What does she know of the skin that must be shed, the pound of flesh exacted in order to do and dare in this world? She opens her bag and takes out a little packet of wafer biscuits. They remind me of communion wafers, pale and refined and textureless. She offers the biscuits to the children, with a tiny crescent smile. They take one each. They are dry, these biscuits, weightless and so dry that they make a crisp, brittle sound when they are eaten, but their religious dryness is itself a form of consolation: the children eat them as I once ate the communion wafer, with its feeling of a dressing on the tongue, a gauze, as though emotion itself were being blotted up. Every few minutes she opens her bag and offers them another. They eat them peacefully. I wish to tell her that it is my fear of separation that has resulted in our presence on this train. I wish to explain to her my belief that it is better to lose houses and friends than to be excluded from your parents' desires. I would say, if we spoke a common language, that it is better to feel pain than not to confront the possibility that you will be hurt; that it is better to commit yourself to the life of knowledge than to cling onto the world of possession.

In the hot afternoon we enter Rome. The train sits there among other trains: the nun gets off. Presently we pull away again. The great city elapses and falls behind. Then we are in green fields that slope down toward the sea. The shoulder of land with its dense green vegetation obscures the probing silvery surf: the blue ancient water makes a simple shape beside the green shape of the fields, and sometimes there are old pink-colored villas standing in a furze of trees that look down on the mystery of the shoreline. Is it possible that Rome is only an hour behind us? We seem so far from anywhere, so remote. This electric-green land hunched around the mineral-colored water: it appears dateless, older than the oldest artifact, older than mountains. A mountain is prolix compared with this place that seems to stand in the dawn of the world's consciousness. The train goes slowly,

in ebbing fits of movement. Then finally it stops altogether, and
for first one hour, then two, we are stranded in the heat until it
seems that we will never move again. The carriage grows hotter.
People move up and down the aisles and hang out of the windows.
We hear that there has been an accident further up the line. We
have no water left. We will disintegrate: we will be broken down
here, slowly erased by the sun and turned to mute and unrecorded
dust, while the sea watches us out of its old blue unblinking eye.

The train starts to move again. The carriage is so hot that our
clothes are soaked with sweat. We gaze silently out of the windows.
We have forgotten the house in the valley, and England, and the
panic of loss: they have been wrung from our minds as the sweat has
been wrung from our bodies. I am glad now that the train stopped,
for I have come to recognize the process of adjustment as a discipline, whose strictures become more binding the longer they are de-
ferred. And it is clear that while we suffered we passed into a different
world: the faces in the train are different, the smell and texture of the
air, the soft, heavy, vitreous light. Just as the children diving for coins
find a place of liberation at the bottom of the pool, so we have discovered a strange freedom at the very root of our intentions.

The air is too hot to breathe. We close our lips and fold up our
lungs, and prepare to swim.

∝

Naples is a city that has the appearance of living among its own
ruins. The great pitted half-derelict terraces crawl with brilliant
life like coral reefs. There are streets like crevasses, dark and
resinous, and streets like canyons that are filthy and beautiful and
grandiose, ravaged across their faces where the walls have here
and there collapsed into rubble. Everywhere there is a feeling of
moisture, the humidity of the life cycle, of birth and decay: the

pavements are heaped with rotting food and rubbish, and the roads are crammed with traffic whose fumes impart their gray, oily cast to the fetid air. Sinuous, lustrous-haired boys and girls fly past like nereids on mopeds; beautiful, tragic women pick their way through the refuse in slender, murderous shoes. And the men, so dark and pagan-looking, so powerful and savagely polite! The men of Naples strike one as absolutely mysterious. They are like little gods, with their air of personal legitimacy, and their fatalistic courtesy that seems to recognize no authority beyond themselves.

I imagine that all cities were once like Naples, in the sense of being alive; an interior sort of life that is beyond the reach of rationality, like that of a bodily organ presiding over its own world of waste and renewal. A bodily organ has no conception of civilization. It is merely programmed to favor life. The virtuous and the malign circulate around its secret ventricles, forever enacting the struggle that is the struggle of all organic things. It is almost shocking to see it, coming from the neutered north. And indeed, even the Italians have warned us about Naples. We have been advised to remove our jewelry, to stuff our money into our underwear. The nereids on mopeds, we have been told, will snatch your purse from your hands as they skim past. They will cheerfully yank the jewels from around your throat and the gold from your ears.

Our *pensione* stands in a dark, moist crease in the innards of a building off the Via Toledo. The black walls are ribbed with narrow iron stairways; far above, the early evening sky lowers a last pale finger of light into the well of gloom. We change our filthy clothes and go out again. It is nearly dark: people are coming out in their finery, their gowns and their glitter, their fancy shoes. Limousines nose through the chaotic streets. The bars are full, the theater is opening its doors. The Piazza Bellini is strung with lights. We walk for a while through the vertiginous, chasm-like streets,

where people converse high up from one side to the other through
the gloaming. I have noticed something, but it has taken me a
while to establish what it is: there are no tourists. There are a few
foreigners, like ourselves, but a foreigner is not the same thing as a
tourist. A foreigner is isolated, observant, displaced. A foreigner
lies low, and takes stock. But a tourist feels at home when he is not.

At last night falls. The darkness is thick and hot and very
black. The World Cup is on, and the restaurants have brought out
their television sets and rigged them up on the pavements. We eat
a pizza and watch the game with the waiters. The children have
gelati. It grows late, but the thick, hot darkness makes it difficult to
think of going to bed. There is a feeling of pause, of stasis. How
can time pass through this thick, resistant matter? The streets are
still full of people. There are tiny children running in the alleyways. The darkness has no quality of intermission. It is like a
blockage. I can't imagine it ever clearing itself to make way for the
dawn. At eleven o'clock we go in, and though I think that I will
never sleep in the gloomy well that has to tunnel up and up before
it can disclose the sky, we wake to find that it is day, that time was
permitted to pass after all and the sun allowed to rise, and that the
smell of *espresso* is creeping like a thief through our open window.

The Museo Archeologico Nazionale is nearby: it stands amid
a great swirl of roads and ruined buildings and whole devastated
tenements showing their foundations like toothless gums. Some
of the ruins have classical shapes. From certain angles the scene
looks like photographs of Berlin after the *blitzkrieg*, and from others like the mystical background of a Leonardo Madonna. The
museum itself is a grand sixteenth-century edifice, as well kept as
any Florentine art gallery, but a significant difference separates
it from the usual haunts of the northern art lover: it is virtually
empty of people. It is ten o'clock in the morning and as far as I can

see we are the only ones here. The lady who takes our tickets in the beautiful modern glass entrance hall looks as delighted to see us as if it had been days since her last visitor; the people in the lavishly furbished cloakrooms want to know everything about our travels and future plans. The curator at the turnstile knows the children's names before they are fully out of their mouths: she strokes their red hair, almost sobbing with pleasure, and admires the drawings in their sketchbooks. Where are the people with suitcases and long lenses, the people in baseball caps and khaki shorts, the scholars and the misfits, the bored teenagers, the tourists fat and thin, the freaks, the fashionable people, the crowds? Where is the cultural ennui? What can the explanation be? Is it possible that they've been scared away by stories of pickpockets on scooters? Do they have so much cash that their underwear can't conceal it? Are they so wedded to their jewelry that they would rather stay at home than leave it behind? Is their aestheticism so shallow, in spite of the hours they spend queuing in its service, that they would rather not come? I find it a little eerie at first, their absence from the sculpture court, from the rooms of the Farnese collection. The Greco-Roman marbles from Pompeii and Herculaneum in the atrium seem to come forth in their strange reality without them there, chewing gum and looking at everything spastically through the lenses of their mobile phones, like earth tourists from outer space. How curious it is, to be here alone! Usually great artworks are so outnumbered by the mob that they seem fragile, almost victimized. But here in the silent, light-filled museum the correctness and cruelty and might of the ancient world is unsheathed.

We wander in the sculpture court, where giant marble limbs and heads and hands lie fallen to the ground and there is a white carved foot the size of a car. Put together, the pieces would make a figure fifty feet high. In 1980 the museum and its collection was badly damaged by the same earthquake that presumably gave its environs their appearance of *blitzkrieg*, though it was not then that the giant fell. Apparently his parts were found buried in the garden of the Villa Farnese. The life of an object is so long, its destruction so heterogeneous. It does not die a single death, like us. It lives on as a hand, a head, a foot. It is buried and reborn. What does it signify, this enormous foot? That man has always been the slave of ambition? It was the restoration work after the earthquake that gave the museum its lavish modern appearance. The earth shook it like a box of sweets, this building full of treasures that had already been drowned in the fire and mud of Vesuvius and resurrected. How murderously it pursued them; and yet the human faculty of love, of patience, that can look on the ruined spectacle of glass and marble and mosaic tiles, all broken and scattered and muddled up, and set about piecing them together again is as strong in its way as violence. This is one reason why the art lover enjoys looking at art. Each object represents another triumph for love, for survival, for care. Each object can be placed on the scales, against man's violence and destructiveness. Which way the scale will tip at the end of it all, nobody knows.

In the atrium there are Aphrodite, Artemis, Athena. I would like to hear their life stories: I would like to know how the world that created them became the world in which they still stand. Their garments fall to their feet in milk-white marble folds; their tapered white fingertips caress the empty air. But their eyes are so blind, so blank: truly, there is death in their unseeing elliptical eyes. It is the death not of themselves but of everything they have looked upon. Their eyes are like mirrors that reflect the void of death. I think of Cimabue, of Giotto, of Duccio's *Maestà* that we saw one day in Siena; of their gilded Madonnas stirring in their painted rigidity, struggling to be born and become mortal. They did not wish to look indifferently on the void of death. They strove to express the authenticity of emotion. Yet they are so unlifelike, compared with these pitiless maidens whose painted eyes time wore effortlessly away, to uncover the annihilating gaze beneath.

Upstairs there are several rooms devoted to the domestic life of Pompeii: everything has been reconstructed, the triclinium and the peristyle, the kitchen with its pots and pans, the dining table with its battered plates and spoons and ashen loaf of bread, as though its owners were about to sit down and eat; as though it were not a place but a moment in time that was captured and sealed in its carapace of volcanic dust. I am struck by the importance of innocence in our view of tragedy. For an incident to satisfy our tragic sense there must have been a predominance of hope over knowledge. There is innocence at the supper table: the loaf of bread, humble though it is, is quintessentially tragic. There are indentations in the risen crust, where the person who made it neatly scored the surface with a knife. The children look at the two-thousand-year-old loaf of bread. I do not think they are marveling at its preservation alone. It is the fact that the bread survived and the people did not that interests them. They would like to taste it. It is almost maddening to them, this triumph of the familiar object. Will the bread never be eaten? Will it just get away with it, for another two thousand years? I myself often make bread, and score the surface with a knife. It is not for this feat that I would like to be remembered, but there is a steadiness to the act that I have noticed many times. There is a feeling of centrality that is directly opposed to the marginal position of the writer of books. Most of all there is a feeling of something lasting, though the bread itself will be eaten soon enough. No, it is not the bread that is the durable object: it is myself, in the act of making it. I am no longer the artist— I am the subject. I am the person in the painting, not the painter. It is strange, that the feeling of immortality should disclose itself in this way, in the prosaic. Nietzsche said that art is what enables us to bear reality. Perhaps what he meant is that it distills the eternal from the everyday and puts it beyond the reach of tragedy.

In the Sale del Tempio d'Iside there are beautiful frescoes, of fruit and flowers and doves preening in a water bath, of men and women, of horses and battles, of gods and satyrs and maenads and scenes from mythology. There are paintings and poems, jewelry and glass vases, erotic cartoons and a beautiful egg poacher, whose beaten metal spheres seem to revolve like the planets of some far-off solar system. There is a whole museum within a museum, the contents of the Villa dei Papiri where Julius Caesar's father-in-law housed his art collection. It is disconcertingly alive, this vanished world of Pompeii. The silent museum seems filled with noise, with faces and glancing eyes and conversation, clattering pots and barking dogs and birdsong. It is as though the volcano did not extinguish the day but took its cast exactly, its sound and smell and atmosphere, its structure, like the skeleton of a fern fossilized in a lump of rock. We go out into the shady courtyard, where a young man gives us glasses of lemon *granita*, diligently, as though he had waited all morning for us to be ready. We sit under a tree. There are one or two other people around, reading books in the shade. Nobody knows we are here. We sit quietly, letting the ice melt a little each time, before we take a sip.

∞

Pompeii is reached from Naples by the Circumvesuviana, a small, gray, graffiti-covered train that looks like it was born in a subway of the Bronx. It charges around the Bay of Naples, through the sprawling conurbations that lie to the south and on to the resorts of the Sorrentine Peninsula, tunneling furiously through poverty and grandeur alike, as though it didn't care for the difference between them. At the stations it flings open its doors, fuming with impatience: the passengers hurl themselves out and the train springs away, rattling helter-skelter past high-rise tenements and Palladian villas, past fragrant glimpses of orange groves, ducking and diving between the volcano and the sea and never pausing too long in the purview of either.

It is very hot, so hot that the plastic bucket seats of the Circumvesuviana are painful to the flesh. If the train stops for more than a few seconds, a feeling of panic sweeps up and down the crowded carriages. At Pompeii we get out and walk along the dusty road in the sun, past the queue of air-conditioned coaches that are disgorging tourists from their sides. There is a little café next to the road, and we sheer off to sit beneath its shady vine and drink Fanta. From our dark corner we scrutinize the crowds. After two and a half months in Italy, we have the demeanor of outlaws when faced with our own kind. And these are the worst, these herds who drive around in coaches, looking numbly down on the world. They are not art lovers. They aren't even really tourists: they are voyeurs.

There is a throng of people at the entrance, but it doesn't take long to get our tickets. I have begun to understand that in Italy a crowd does not necessarily represent an obstacle to desire. Much of the time, people amass for reasons of their own. They queue because they want to, or because their relationship with the thing they are queuing for is insufficiently direct. Often the people standing in a queue will all be queuing for entirely different things. Then there are the people who can never believe that they are in the *right* queue, who continually ask their neighbors what the queue is for and send waves of unrest up and down its length. And there are those who seem to queue solely for the feeling of security it gives them, as though it is only in the queue that they are truly safe from another fresco, another Madonna, another Donatello head, about which they might be compelled to give an opinion, or

fail to feel something they were told they should. The Italians re-
spond to this dissociative behavior with the utmost cordiality.
Nothing summons their compassion more readily than a devital-
ized tourist, and their sympathy grows in direct proportion to its
object's lack of charm. It is as though the thing they pity most in
all the world is ugliness.

We pass through the gates and out into the cauldron of afternoon. The integuments of the ancient town, diagrammatic, skeletal,
pure as bone, rise and extend in terraces all around: everywhere the
force of extension drives toward its own vanishing point, for the town
is flat, radial, starlike, with few upright walls to arrest the driving force
of the straight line toward the horizon. The effect is ghostly: the
volcano, so pyramidal in mass and shape, so grossly upright, lowers over the prostrated, map-like town. It is corpulent where the
town is abstracted. It has devoured it, and left the bones. Yet there is
something religious about the driving symmetry of the lines, the
mathematical stepping and extending of the ruined terraces into
space. There is a system, an order, a plan. The volcano is a mere
beast. The plan, the mathematical essence of civilization, defies it.

The tourists are delighted with their new home: they stroll and
chatter in the deep-ridged streets, they pass in and out of doorways, they minuet at corners and crossroads, now deferential, now
proprietorial, as though they had donned its social hierarchy like
a fancy-dress toga. The forum is filled with its rightful bustle; people come and go at the bakery and the baths. It is a shame they
can't live here, they seem to like it so. Sometimes, in a shady corner, a glass case is to be found with a rough gray shape lying inside:
these are the casts the volcanic ash cruelly made of its victims, to
immortalize their helplessness. They are crude and barely human;
they are like primitive clay figures. Yet their blurred, blank quality
is disturbing. It is somehow more embryonic than deathly. We stand

around the glass cases sadly, as though their contents only needed
our compassion to humanize them again. The inexactitude of the
figures: how mysterious and elusive it is, when their pots and pans
and egg poachers have come down to us unharmed. There is an
atmosphere of guilt around them. The cases are shabby, and filled
with grit. Could they not be resting on something more comfortable? They seem so unloved, lying there in their strangely unfinished, unborn state.

The day grows hotter; the volcano is cloaked in haze; in the
distance the blue sea lies passive, recessed, a strange fluorescence
pulsing on its surface. The crowds seem to grow more and more
excited. They seem a little crazed. They seem overexposed. They
rush hither and thither like children playing hide-and-seek. They
barge and tread on one another's feet. They shove and yell in
the amphitheater, beneath the smiting sun. There is a group of
German students, handsome and extravagantly dressed, who are
following their professor around the ruins. They are tall and flam-

*The Catechism with a Young Girl Reading and the Initiate Making an Offering,
North Wall, Oecus 5*, c. 60–50 B.C. (fresco), by Roman

boyant and unreal-seeming, like actors on a film set, like people in *The Great Gatsby*. Their professor has a messianic appearance, in his white flannel suit. I notice them, for they ask to be noticed. Amid the heat and the ruins they have the carved, mocking quality of gods. Later, in the Villa dei Misteri, we see them again. The professor is chanting something in German, a strange, sonorous, interminable recitative that echoes all through the sepulchral rooms. Every now and again the students chant back to him in chorus. We cannot escape it, this mad Wagnerian oratory: the sound is sinister, almost frightening, as though a new cult were being hatched from the blood-soaked soil. We pass through room after room, taunted by the unbodied voices. Finally we come upon them, standing in the blood-red triclinium before the fresco of the Mysteries. The fresco shows a young girl being initiated into the cult of Dionysus. I might have found it beautiful had I been alone, for the girl's mother rests her hand on her daughter's shoulder and curls her fingers unconsciously around the tresses of her hair. The mystery and brutality of the pre-Christian world might have remained theoretical; the subject might have escaped me, as it generally does escape the art lover, in the face of the belief in art as an ultimate good.

But the messianic master stands before it, chanting. He is terrible, exultant, malign. His students gaze at him with trancelike expressions. Their eyes are the blank, elliptical eyes of marble goddesses.

∝

We have booked a room in Piano di Sorrento. The man at the door bows courteously at our arrival. He introduces himself: he is Paolo. He is so small and dapper and cool. We are so hot, and rimed with pumice dust. The door from the street, where the air-conditioned coaches thunder along the narrow road to Sorrento, was deceiving: behind it there is a garden, green and shady, with peaches growing on the trees.

All the same, we are a little shocked by the change of climate: by the heat, the frenzy, the crowded precipitate hillsides plunging down into the sea, the pell-mell succession of the squalid and the sublime, the feeling everywhere of cramp, of confinement, of the imprecision of desire meeting the exactitude of possibility. We go down to the beach at Castellammare to swim: it is so crowded on the narrow gritty stretch that the children have to sit on our laps amid the cigarette butts, and in the rubbish-strewn water it's standing room only. The bus can barely squeeze back up the narrow road. The cars inch past one another, snagging on the hairpin bends. This is a world so vertical that the horizontal is a form of luxury. I sit on the bus with my eyes shut, dreaming of prairies, of my flat East Anglian childhood.

It is Paolo's ancestral home that we are staying in. Once it was quiet here, on a hilltop above the sea, but now the house is impacted in the vertical tundra of development that covers the whole northern coast of the peninsula. It is not particularly ugly, this modern geology. It is just that in its fundamental properties it has the qualities of an anxiety dream. Paolo shows us the family chapel, a light, whitewashed little room on the first floor whose windows look out on the rooftops and the community football pitch. There is a plaster statue of the red-cheeked Virgin, and spindly wooden chairs in rows, facing the altar. He shows us the dining room and the suite of drawing rooms, with their gold brocade sofas and family portraits and great ceramic urns standing in the shadows. The shutters are closed against the sun. The marble floors are silent underfoot. It is like a museum, except that the present moment is checked at the front door. The world does not flow around these objects: instead there is Paolo, attenuated and leather-skinned, faintly saturnine, with his small, polished, bony head like the head on a Roman coin. Paolo's wife comes in. She is a Veronese madonna, yellow-haired, decked in gold, rather excitable, who moves rapidly in a shoal of little dogs. She tells us that they have just had a grand wedding here. It was their daughter who was married. Things are a little chaotic, a little mad. The house is upside down. She asks how long we are staying, and what we have been doing: she shudders at the mention of Pompeii. She herself is from the north. She doesn't like it here, in this cacophonous dust bowl under the volcano. Most of the time she and Paolo live in Rome.

In the evening we take the bus along the coast. The sun is going down, and the sky flames with pink. The sea is soft and silent, with a milk-white sheen. An eerie calmness settles on the belle époque villas on their promontories of rust-colored rock when the light leaves their faces. They take on strange, savage shapes, with their plumes of palm trees and dilapidated balustrades. A drift of lights heaps itself around the bay. Over the water we can see Naples, smoking like a mound of embers. The cone of the volcano is dark, effaced, as though these lights were rivers of lava it had discharged itself. We get off the bus and walk down through a dank staircase in the rock, all the way down through the cliff until we come out far below, beside the water. There is a tiny beach, and a jetty. There is nobody here. We take off our clothes and jump off the jetty into the water. The water is warm, silky: it seems not to wet us but to coat us with its milky sheen. It is a relief, at last, to swim, but the water withholds something from us. It has the same impenetrable quality as everything else, a feeling of mystery, almost of secrecy, as though it were not fully present to us. It is half violated, this beautiful bay with its rubbish-strewn water and shroud of polluted air. It is like a violated woman who refuses to give up her secret.

We walk back up through the cliff and sit down in the restaurant at the top. It has a round terrace that abuts the precipice. Gulls land on the balustrade and look sharply at the tourists through the dusk. There are English people here, middle-aged men and women with brick-red skin who say please and thank you in their native tongue, for it is easier to be transported to the Bay of Naples than to form the sounds that compose the word *grazie*. The men sit silently with their pints of lager, their beefy red arms folded across their chests. The women are silent too. They hold their handbags on their laps and take tiny sips from their glasses of sherry. They seem to disapprove of something, in their neat blouses and skirts, their rigid helmets of hair. They look down on the violated woman succumbing to her trance of night. In their way they have a deep secrecy of their own. Is it their own bodies they disapprove of, for being transported here? At least their minds remain theirs, refusing to say *buongiorno* and *grazie*. What are their bodies, that they can just be lifted out of one place and set down in another? Where will they find themselves next? The waiters are exquisitely gentle with these people. They refill the pint glasses at the merest nod. They straighten the nearby tables and chairs so that the deracinated bodies will not be buffeted or bruised. They like them: I have been told this by Italians, how much they like the English. They don't care what language the please and thank you come in. Apparently most Italians never say thank you at all. The word is like a pearl, falling from those reticent English lips. It is clear that the waiters will stop at nothing to prize out as many of them as they can.

∝

The next day we go down to the harbor at Sorrento, to take the boat to Capri. But there is no boat to Capri: the boatmen are on

strike. We pace about the harbor fretfully, conferring. The town lies above in its fortress of rock. It is full of big, brassy hotels and souvenir shops and red-skinned tourists. Beyond it lies the green headland and beyond that the sea. I had wanted to go to Capri: I had decided on it as the turning point in our travels, the gold coin at the bottom of the pool that I needed to grasp to be released. It had seemed important to me, to touch it, to grasp it. How else could I understand our experiences unless I gave them a shape, an arc? Standing in the hot, crowded harbor, I feel my artistry being unpicked. I feel my conception faltering, breaking up. I feel the question forming itself, the question that has not yet been asked, that I meant never to be asked again: What are we doing here?

A man approaches. He tells us that there is a boat, a single boat that will take us around the headland to Positano, on the Amalfi coast. I do not particularly want to go to Positano. I want to go to Capri. I want to see the Carthusian monastery, and Tiberius's villa. I want to go to an island, from where I can look back on the last three months and make the decisive stroke that will complete them. It will be no good, going to Positano. It will be artificial. It will not be satisfying. It will ruin everything with its artificiality, its lack of truth. Nevertheless, we get on the boat. There is, after all, nowhere else to go. We have come to the end. I will not go back up to Sorrento and stare through the windows of souvenir shops beneath the hammering sun. It is preferable to be on the water, in limbo, chugging around the headland to get to the other side. From Positano we can take a bus back over the middle to Paolo's. It will be a little circle. It will be tourism for halfwits, for imbeciles.

The boat trip takes an hour. We watch the green-tufted headland; we watch the sea. We see Capri, dimly, through the polluted haze. Now and then huge speedboats roar by, or skirmish in their own foam. Positano comes into view, and steadily advances across the bobbing water. Its pink and white houses climb steeply up the hillside in the sun. The shore is full of bodies. They lie, basking like lizards. They watch our approach through their countless pairs of sunglasses. The whole spectacle seems to move up and down, though it is the boat that moves. But the town seems unhinged, unfixed. It seems like a figment of someone's imagination.

We get off. The children fling away their shoes and run onto the dark, gritty sand. Then they turn round and run straight back, alarmed. The sand is so hot it has burned their feet. And it seems we must pay to be on the beach. It is fifteen euros each. We stand at the fence and look into the ranks of loungers and parasols where the community basks inscrutable behind its sunglasses. The heat is infernal; the torpid water rolls noiselessly on the shore. We have been trapped, cornered. The boat chugs away across the water; far above the road scribbles among the hilltops. We are seized suddenly by bravado: we pay the money and establish ourselves in the front row, among the millionaires and divas and the honeymooning couples. We flick up our parasol; we buy lemon ices in tall glasses; we don our sunglasses and examine our neighbors with unconscionable thoroughness.

There is a couple nearby, American, young and blond and groomed as gods. The boy has the faux-heroic look of a Kennedy, with his snub patrician face and sculpted nimbus of hair. The girl is classical, farouche as a Jamesian heroine: she discloses her body in its spotless white swimming costume shyly, like a marble nymph. The boy's costume is white too. They look like brother and sister, though it is clear they are on honeymoon. They lie side by side on their loungers, glancing around self-consciously, estranged somehow, in spite of their common aesthetic purpose. It is as though they are impersonating a pair of rich East Coast newlyweds, but there is no reason to think that that is not what they are. The boy gets up and goes alone into the sea. He swims out a little way and then returns and hangs just offshore. He keeps his head above the water. He tosses his hair. Then the girl comes to the water and steps carefully in. She is so self-conscious she can barely swim. She is as though very old, or ill. She reaches the boy and half embraces him in the water. I see him avert his face: he is worried she will wet his hair. He pushes her away, sending her back to shore. Then for a long time he stays out there, tossing his hair this way and that, so frantically that I wonder whether he is mad. The girl sits on her lounger with a strange little smile on her face.

The children play in the water; the sun is high, and the sea is a furnace of glitter. The light seems to liquidize everything, the · people and the parasols, the boats and houses and green hills behind. They grow molten, indistinct. Only sound is left, the sucking of the sea, the drone of voices, the shrieks of gulls and the distant thrumming of engines. I close my eyes and the question is there. What am I doing here? It is as though I have carried a picture in my mind that has suddenly been atomized, has separated into a million particles. In its place there is the world, atonal, indiscriminate, random. It is late June. Tomorrow we are turning round. We are starting our journey home. But I have broken something here, on the journey's floor, at its southernmost point. Something has been mislaid. I open my eyes and there is the honeymooning couple. Did they steal it from me, the feeling of understanding? For though I look and look at them I can make no sense of them at all. I need Raphael to paint them for me. I need an artist, to refine crude life into something I can understand.

Later we take the bus back, along the inland road that winds through the mountains. The settlements of the coast vanish behind a bend. There is only the sky above and the sea below. It is so green up here, so wild. It seems to exult in its own freedom. We pass through out-of-the-way places where women hang their clothes on washing lines. Then we are in green again, in tangled thickets that run freely up and over the peaks, run beneath the dome of the sky. The water seems to watch them from below, these wild hills. It watches them like a mother watches a running child. It embraces their feet. It seems, somehow, to be smiling.

ROMAN TALES

It is the World Cup quarterfinal. Italy are playing. This event courses through the geology of old Rome as evening falls, like a wave breaking into a cove and rushing through its fissures and crevices, briefly filling its twisted, ancient gulleys of rock. The cafés put out their television sets. People form deltas on the pavements at the mouths of crowded bars. The cars backed up in the narrow streets blare their horns, streamers hanging from their windows. In the Piazza Navona boys are detonating canisters of colored smoke. They skirmish on their Vespas, naked to the waist, brandishing flags whose flowing drapery and long poles impart the final classicism to their painterly forms, so that they look like figures in a battle scene, forever skirmishing in the blue fog of war. The Pantheon and the Colosseum and the Palatine Hill are not insensible to this modern kind of frenzy, for they give it form. They are refreshed by it, as the rock is refreshed by the wave. Nevertheless, the city retains a core of obliviousness. There are still people wandering around with suitcases, people staring into shopwindows, people consulting maps in the last light. There is a woman lying in a doorway, unconscious, covered in mud. There are waiters standing on the thresholds of empty restaurants. There are tourist families sitting at brightly lit tables, a little awkward-looking, as though they are surprised and slightly disappointed to find themselves unaltered, sitting around a table exactly as they do at home. The hot, motionless, indigo-colored evening passes into an annihilated blackness, like something burning out. Now and again the din of rockets and car horns and klaxons is suddenly ignited all across the city. Italy have scored another goal.

We stay out late, until the game has finished and the crowds dispersed and the cars and Vespas are blazing like comets up and down the Via Nazionale proclaiming victory, shrieking past in a shower of horns and lights. On the bus the other passengers seem mysterious, inscrutable, distinguished: when they speak, their Italian is so formal and correct that it is difficult to understand. Their faces are ancient and aristocratic. Though the night is hot they are attired with lavish sobriety, like royalty. Their eyes seem to be looking at great distances within themselves. These are Romans: they are quite different from the other Italians we have observed. They have a certain proud Travertine stillness about them, a monumental quality. They seem quintessentially European; they are a kind of race. "Rome is inhabited by know-nothings who do not want to be disturbed," Federico Fellini once remarked. "The Roman is like a grotesque, overgrown child who has the satisfaction of being continually spanked by the Pope." And indeed, not so long ago Rome's infamy had something of the quality of metaphor. Endowed and tainted to the core, it seemed to express an ultimate cynicism that could outpace any human attempt at nobility. It was the capital city of corruption and pollution and hypocrisy, of unbecoming gropings on public transport. But now even the *mano morta* is no more: apparently the Roman male keeps his hands to himself. An Italian told us that the phenomenon ceased a few years ago. She could give no reason why: it just stopped. It was, perhaps, the Italian capacity for evolution that caused this unfashionable trait to be so abruptly discarded. In this city, where time does not pass so much as refine itself, analyze itself, questions of being and behavior may become entirely psychical. It would be possible, I think, to have no conscience at all, if you walked past the Colosseum and the Forum each day. It would be in the psyche, the root, that actions were decided.

The bus passes the Palazzo Barberini and emerges into the broad, flat distances of the Via XX Settembre. In the charred darkness the lit-up buildings look like monsters, or ghosts. We are staying a little way out of the center, in a small hotel that is reached through its own garden, where birds dart from the hedges and the other guests sit here and there in the shade, their eyes closed and their hands folded in their laps, as though the birds and the green garden and the city beyond it are things they are dreaming. Our room is at the top, in the eaves. The ancient lift rises slowly through the center of the stairwell, so that people walking up and down can be seen through its glass panels. On the way down the children generally take the stairs, running round and round us in our glass capsule, laughing and waving at us through the banisters. This activity never fails to amuse them. It strikes me that they find in it a reversal of the usual order of things, for though we all take the same course, in general it is we who are free and they enclosed in the mystery of our plans. Their excitement is tinged with anxiety: what would happen if the lift got stuck, and they could see us but not reach us? At home they are not conscious of such fears, but here, in a foreign city in a foreign land, in a labyrinth of separation whose twists and turns did not end at Newhaven but rather began there, so that the original separation could never be found in all the relinquished affection that has followed it—here their bond to us is strong, with not an inch of slack. Later, back in England, they speak constantly of Italy, even when the months away have been matched fivefold by those since our return. They say that Italy is where they would

most like to live in the whole world. They say that as soon as they
are grown up, they are going back to the valley and the *castello*, forever. They will buy a farm, or perhaps the house itself. When they
speak like this they remind me of the characters in Italo Svevo's
A Life, of the hero Alfonso, whose experience of love and belong-
ing could not be disentangled from his mother and the valley where
he grew up. For the children, the sensory experience of Italy was
fused with uninterrupted proximity to their parents, and so they
wish to return there, even though in their fantasy they are now the
adults and we are absent. Yet I recall the pain they felt at the time,
of having left their friends and home behind, the pain of knowledge: this, it appears, was entirely distinct from their love of the
place in which they now found themselves. Back in England, the
memory of Italy does not cause them pain. They feel a longing
that is more fundamental, that is the preference of their souls.
They have been formed, not bereaved, that much is clear.

In the morning we walk, skulking on the fringes of the tourist
crowds. The city is hot, packed, turbid, with a faintly volcanic
scent of rocks and dust. The barging traffic releases its fumes,
shimmering and nacreous, into the hazy sky. We wander in the dry
gardens of the Villa Borghese, along the fine dirt paths. We visit
the Trevi Fountain, hidden in its network of narrow alleyways like
an idea flowering secretly in the dank network of the brain. Its
white, fanciful extravagance has been found out, like the sick rose
in Blake's poem. It is crawling with people, whose clothes and bags
and camera equipment look malevolent, arachnoid, against the
foaming white. We visit the Roman Forum, the great decaying
cavity splayed out, dissected-looking, under the sun. People clamber in the rubble with their cameras: some of them move in big,
indifferent groups behind their guides, and some are in couples,
quietly conferring, a faintly strained air about them, as though the

whole civilized enterprise of their union is under threat from the shock of the unruly past; as though it is the future that has decayed and vanished and abandoned them here, in the ravaged Forum in their Gucci sunglasses and expensive shoes.

We climb up the Palatine Hill and then emerge out into a deserted backstreet. It is silent here, blank: now and again a person comes out as we came out, unexpectedly, as though falling from a dream. They pass us, looking around in bewilderment, and disappear. After a while we walk on, through one empty street and then another. We come out on the Capitoline Hill and enter the Palazzo Nuovo of the Capitoline Museum. There are few people inside, though the world's richest collection of Roman art and relics is here. It is cool and quiet, eternal. Outside there is a feeling of eternity too, except that it is an eternity of repetition, of the same moment being lived over and over again, day after day, as people see the landmarks of Rome for the first time; always new people doing exactly the same thing, just as the water that runs ceaselessly over a rock in a riverbed is always new. But inside the museum it is as deep and still as a lake. We sit motionless in the window seats of the sculpture rooms on the first floor. We stare at Aphrodite and Venus and Eros, at Homer and Hercules, and they return our stares. They are so white and hard and perfect, so aloof. Their forms are so familiar that they seem like fellow creatures, yet we belong to the perishable race that runs in its endlessly renewing moment over the riverbed. The children are exhausted and dumb. Today they cannot accept the discipline of art. Their skin is brown and they wear patterned cotton scarves tied around their hair. Their feet in their sandals are dusty. We show them the sculpture of the little girl with the dove; we show them the *Spinario*, the boy pulling a thorn from his foot. These frozen images glimmer in the underwater light of the museum. It makes no difference that they

are images of children: today they emanate only perfection and
death.

We go upstairs, up and up to the roof, where there is a café.
The café is crowded, but beyond its doors there is a beautiful terrace, immense and open to the sky, with all of Rome lying beneath
it. There are tables and white cloths and silverware out there, and
urns of flowers, and a smart canvas sun canopy, but the tables are
empty. People are standing at the windows of the thronged café as
though imprisoned, looking longingly out. We pass through the
doors and out onto the terrace, where there is a sign. It says that
people sitting at these tables must be served by a waitress. We con-
sult the menu: the food is the same out here as in there; there is no
extra charge. It is merely, it seems, a matter of procedure, or personal taste. It suggests that some people dislike being served by a
waitress; but never have we wanted anything more. We sit, and
presently she comes, a plump girl with beautiful black hair in a
maidenly roll, and an expression of sweetness and simplicity, like
Correggio's Virgin. She takes our order; she unfurls our napkins
and gently smooths the children's scarves over their hair. Behind
her, people have seen us sitting at our table and started to spill out
of the café, carrying their trays. She informs them sweetly that
they are not permitted to sit out here, though she doesn't explain
why. She disappears and returns again, bringing iced water and *ce-
drata* for the children, then tiny delicious sandwiches and *gelati*, and
each time our glorious solitude is threatened she drives them back
inside with not a word of explanation. We order *espresso* and she
brings it carefully with almond *biscotti*. Now and again a breeze lifts
from the rooftops like an ocean swell, and the flowers nod their
heads. We can see a hundred domes, the dome of St. Peter's and
the broad brown Tiber, the oceanic rise and fall of hills, the
strange, catastrophic tilt of human history, the field of stone like a

million intricate husks of endeavor and belief. The sky is tinted pink where it meets the rust-red roofs, as though over time a little of the dye had rubbed off on its blue. The Correggio Virgin brings a little dish of wrapped chocolates for the children to the table and offers us more *espressi*. She gives us a mysterious rosebud smile, and turns to straighten the cloths and silver on the empty tables.

∞

We walk through the hot bruise-colored evening down the Spanish Steps, past the Pantheon and through the Piazza Navona, where an Egyptian pharaoh stands in the gloaming, motionless in his synthetic gold sheath. He has been standing there all day, beneath the smiting sun. Now the last tourists drift by, to look at him and see if he will move: he doesn't. They drop coins into a bowl at his feet. After a while, once darkness has fallen, his hands appear from within the sheath and he removes his mask. He steps down from the box concealed beneath the gold material. He lifts the sheath over his head. He is a small man, mustached, Middle Eastern, wearing a faded Nike T-shirt. He packs everything away, and counts the coins in his bowl.

We cross the river and pass into the Trastevere, with its air of genteel squalor and monitored bohemianism. At a bar we stop and order glasses of pale wine. We sit for a while and watch other people. There is a big group at a nearby table, two or three families, the adults around our own age. They are Italians. They look prosperous, intelligent, carelessly attractive: they have a number of children and dogs. They are laughing, talking; more people come and they embrace them and laugh and talk even louder. One of them has her shopping in a basket at her feet. I can see tomatoes, a sheaf of basil, a stick of bread. They are so settled, so established.

We watch them and drink our drinks. Have we tired of our root-
lessness? Do we want friends, pets, establishment?

Two things have happened. The first is more of a dawning, a realization, than a happening: we have nearly run out of money. The
second is a realization too, in its way, but it feels like an event. It is
that we have changed. The change is hard to quantify, to accommodate, for it makes itself apparent only in the fact that we are neither
tourists nor citizens, and however spiritually relieving that fact might
be, it is difficult to know how to live in the world in the light of it.
The longer we stay in Italy, the less we are able to conduct ourselves
like visitors. Yet to live here, really live, would involve the same
things as living anywhere. There would be school and routine, anxiety and conformity, judgment and separation, success and failure.
There would be all the ripples of effect that are sent out when
people establish themselves among other people. Is it these ripples,
these imperceptible chains, that we shrink from sending forth? To
live in another country requires a fundamental acceptance of
things that are true in all countries. I have known people who have
moved abroad, by choice rather than compulsion: the majority of
them, before they leave, assert at every opportunity the ways in
which their prospective homeland is better, and once they are
there insist with equal vehemence on the ways in which it is worse.
As a child, my parents were constantly moving. They, too, seemed
to believe that when they moved, the bad things would remain behind. And perhaps they did: but the good things stayed there also.

I do not want to relocate, to stay, to settle down. I want to
roam, like the writers and artists of an earlier age with their fashionable selfishness. D. H. Lawrence, for instance, lived everywhere, at least for the time it took him to come to hate the place.
In *Sea and Sardinia* he describes an ocean voyage and two-week
visit to Sardinia that he and his wife Frieda made one winter from

Sicily, where they lived at the time. Sardinia is cold, austere, beautiful but a little cheerless, and their stay there is relatively brief. Nevertheless, Lawrence is constantly exhorting himself and his disconsolate companion to decide one way or the other: Could they live there? It seems he could go nowhere without ascertaining its fitness to sustain life, like a scientist scanning distant planets for signs of water and oxygen. Frieda, who had left her three young children in order to live with Lawrence, and caused such a scandal thereby that she was forbidden from ever seeing or contacting them, must truly have felt herself to be far inside the labyrinth of separation, every new move cutting her ties with England, though Sardinia was no further away than Sicily. Lawrence, perhaps, wanted to sever Frieda from her past, with its rival mother-love, but in every new place they went, her longing for her children was there. How many places would you have to move before you forgot who you were?

Lawrence himself tired of Italy, its little gardenlike landscapes, its art that he began to see as a substitute for life, its soppiness, what he called its "macaroni love." He claimed to appreciate Sardinia for its lack of culture: how pleasant, he wrote, to come to a place where there were no Peruginos you had to go and look at. There was a time when he had needed to look at Peruginos, and also to enter the Roman past, the Hellenic. He had needed to furnish his soul with classicism, but he had outlived that need. Now what he required was life itself, living humanity. In *The Rainbow* Lawrence writes of the operation of culture as a form of grace in human evolution. People discover books, art, music; they inch forward in consciousness, pass on their discoveries to their children, who inch forward a little more. In *The Rainbow*, Will Brangwen is a frustrated aesthete who believes he will create art, but who ends up a bitter, violent man, teaching carpentry at adult-education classes in the new socially inclusive England of the early twentieth century. It is his daughter, Gudrun, who becomes the artist and thereby escapes her regional, working-class roots. Will, as the father of young children, would sit in the Nottinghamshire evenings leafing through his precious art books with their reproductions of Fra Angelico, but it was his daughter who would consummate his desire for these images. Will is able to comprehend beauty but not to bear its caste. As a man he is cruel, and fettered by upbringing. In the end the Fra Angelicos fail to refine his nature.

I am half shocked by Lawrence's remarks about art, but I sympathize with them too. He did not, after all, know how physically ugly the world would become. For me, it is necessary to look at Perugino, in order to digest the supermarkets and shopping malls, the litter and landfill sites, the pylons and traffic jams and motorway service stations that otherwise fill the eye. Without beauty, the human sensibility becomes discouraged. One could look at a flower, of course, or a child; but to look at a painting is to feel looked at, comprehended, yourself. It is to experience empathy, for what is art but the struggle to acknowledge the fact that we ourselves were created? Over time the morality of art has become clear and distinct: we don't ask it to be correct, or selfless, or didactic, or judgmental. We don't blame it for the uses to which it is put. We don't expect it to intervene, to determine, to make peace or war, to end poverty or greed, to abate suffering. We ask only that it be beautiful and true. We turn to it to dignify our experience of the world; to find a reply to the question of consciousness.

But I, too, have a qualm about the Fra Angelicos, the Peruginos. It is that they belong to the past. Their reality is so remote from our own: I fear that to look at them is a form of nostalgia. I fear the feeling of sadness they cause me, sadness that our own world is not more beautiful. I wonder whether the others feel that

too, queuing down the streets in their thousands, thronging at the
ropes of museums.

∾

It is our last day in Rome: we are going to Vatican City. We have
left it a little late to scale this peak, the Vatican museums with their
seven kilometers of exhibits, the Sistine Chapel and the Raphael
Stanze, the Borgia apartments, the Etruscan galleries. We have let
time slip away from us, as sleep slips away from those who dwell
too much on what the day will bring. We have begun to worry
about the future, and the present has strayed from our clutches.

It is very hot, and I have hurt my foot. The pain is in the arch, a
strange, screwlike agony that radiates a secondary numbness, so that
my leg feels like a block of wood. It has been there for several days,
though I have tried to deny it. My pace of walking has merely got
slower and slower: the others stop and look round, finding that I am
not there. For a while there was a mute adaptation to these new circumstances, as though we had been unexpectedly joined on holiday
by an invalid great-aunt, who limped stoically in the rear. The children have started wincing and apologizing when they step by accident on my foot, causing me to shriek. When we sit down at a café,
they automatically drag over an extra chair, for me to put my leg on.
But on our last day in Rome, the veil of denial is torn down. It is
ridiculous. I can barely walk. We must do something: we must act.

I refuse the doctor and the hospital point-blank. I will see the
Raphael Stanze, no matter how much it hurts. To go to the doctor
would take all day. Instead we will go to the pharmacy. But the
pharmacy near the hotel is shut. We ask a passerby the reason: it is
Sunday. She thinks it will open for a short while at eleven. We sit
on a bench and wait. It is pleasant to sit down in the shade. It is all
I can think about, how pleasant it is. This is not because I am tired:

it is because the pain, when I stand, is unbearable. When I look down at my foot I notice it is swollen. I worry, vaguely, about the time: our Vatican hours are being steadily consumed. If only I could stay on the bench, all would be well. I imagine the others pushing me on it around the museum, while I lie on my back and gaze upward at the Sistine Chapel.

At last the pharmacy opens. The pharmacist touches my foot and I shriek. She gives me painkillers, and a tube bandage like a thick white sock. She does not involve herself in what the matter might be: she's only a pharmacist. She does not have the doctor's duty, to bring the crimes of the body to justice. I intend to get away with it, and she is my accessory. For a while, on the bus, I am buoyant. The bandage has a placebo effect: when I held it in my hands in the pharmacy, my foot seemed to speak. It affirmed that the bandage was what it needed. It throbbed with belief. But the truth is that the bandage makes no difference at all. When I put it on, it was like putting on a sweater to address a stomachache. There was a moment of disjointure, of failure to connect, before the pain thrummed on, resuming its separate journey. It has a masklike virtue, at least. It makes what lies beneath it more horrible to me, but more bearable for everyone else.

The bus arrives at Vatican City. There is a walk, short enough, but deep in its dimension of agony. When we reach the Piazza San Pietro I look up, and in my vulnerable state its blinding white vastness seems awful and ominous. It is as huge and cold and hostile as a glacier. These are the pilgrim spaces, these gigantic man-made voids—the piazza is said to be able to hold three hundred thousand people with ease—but to me they are inhuman and terrifying. The piazza is rounded at its open end. It is meant to be shaped like a shell. But there is nothing shell-like about it at all. A shell is small and delicate. If a shell were the size of the Piazza San Pietro,

it would belong in a horror film, a monstrous bivalve that ram-
paged around the world, shovelling three hundred thousand people at a time into its scalloped jaws.

I limp across the white, diamond-hard expanse, trailing after
the others. It is midday, and the sun is ferocious. With my limp and
my bandage I could be a true pilgrim, come to St. Peter's to be
healed. I have always been somewhat afraid of the pilgrim character. When I was fourteen, I went to Lourdes with my convent school
to assist the pilgrimage of sick people from England. We took the
boat and then the overnight train. I shared a carriage with a man
whose wife was dying from cancer. She lay in her bunk, a swollen
woman with terrible coarse threads of hair trailing from her bald
scalp. The train rocked, and pulsed continually with its shuttered
yellow light. Her face was grotesquely enlarged; she groaned, and
sometimes flailed helplessly in her sheet. It was as though she had
discovered something awful, on the very edge of life. Her husband
thought she might not survive the journey to Lourdes and back.
He said so, repeatedly. The train was so pell-mell, so indifferent. It
sped through the night, rocking, as though it would stop for nothing. I tended numerous women during that week in the Lourdes
hospital. Their bodies were so contorted, so satirized. It made
death seem like an unpleasant kind of joke. There was mockery, as
though of the sincerity with which they had lived in their own
flesh. One of them had gangrene in her leg. We became friendly:
I had to clip her blackened toenails, both of us shaking with laughter. On the boat on the way home there was a storm in the English
Channel, and I remember empty wheelchairs pitching up and
down the corridors, and the sound of groaning that came and went
as the cabin doors swung back and forth on their hinges.

We pass in front of St. Peter's, where Mass is being said, and
people are queuing to have their bags examined by the security

guards. Then we sheer off into a narrow street that runs beneath the high Vatican walls to the museums. It is shady here and the children run ahead, leaping up in the coolness like water leaps in a fountain. The walk is long. My foot aches, but I don't care quite so much. It is enough, to be in this quiet, shady street away from the blinding white tundra of the pilgrim square; to be alone, ourselves, in Italy, with no God to beg from or placate, with the Raphael Stanze and the Sistine Chapel before us. The children run ahead and come back, run ahead and come back. Tomorrow we are leaving, going north. But we will still be together.

I sit down on the curbstone, underneath the high wall. It seems that I can go no further. The others stand and look down at me. I perceive their consternation in vague, shadowy blocks with the sun behind like a halo. Then they say that they will go on to ascertain the length of the queue, while I rest here. They go, and a short time later they return. There is no queue. The museums are closed on Sundays. We should have checked: we are losing our touch. We have missed our chance.

For a while we stay where we are, idling on the pavement in the shade. I think of Alberto Moravia's stories, the *Roman Tales*, where disappointment is always the springboard to some kind of truth, a truth that lies beyond desire and motivation. The others sit on a bench. I remain on the curbstone. Presently my daughter takes a photograph of me. I look at it sometimes, back in England. I am a woman of thirty-nine, casually dressed, with a white bandage on her foot. The place where I sit, in the right angle of the curb and the wall, is so old that the stones have been worn into rounded shapes. In a minute I am going to get up: I won't be there anymore. It is almost as though I am not there at all. It is the stones that are really there, not me. Maybe one day I'll go back and sit in the same place, to prove something. But all the same, I look happy. I am smiling.

IN THE WOODS

We have a tent. It is Tiziana's: she lent it to us. Before we left to go south, she erected it for us on the grassy slope of her garden, beside the wooden hut. It is a small tent, dome-shaped, faded blue on the outside, with a faded pink interior. The bleached colors are intimate: it is Tiziana's use that has faded them. We all get inside, while Tiziana's huge black dogs lie down on the hot grass at the flap. It is like sitting in a shell, or a teacup. The brilliant afternoon disappears: the tent is filled with a diffuse, rose-colored light, and the unbodied sounds of outside, of the dogs panting softly in the heat. Tiziana strokes the worn material, recalling her travels. She has been happy in this tent. She has taken it with her everywhere. She wishes to bequeath it to us, this frail shelter that can simply be unfolded and become a place, as familiar as a room, then cease to exist again. She doesn't like the thought of it ceasing to exist. We promise to send it when we get back to England, but Tiziana shrugs. She doesn't think she'll be camping anytime soon, dug in as she is on Jim's doorstep, awaiting an opportunity to strike.

It is July, and the summer lies heavy on the landscape; the heat extends everywhere, across night and day, unbroken. We pick up the car in Arezzo and drive to the coast, past the port of Piombino with its ships and steel foundries and boats to Elba, out across the deserted countryside of the headland, and north to remote Populonia and the Gulf of Baratti. The light is dry, ancient, on the earth-colored shoreline. The sea is a sheet of glitter. The tufted green headland, the grassy dunes with their crescent of pine trees, the brown-hillocked mystery of the Etruscan necropolis that stands beside the water, the fortified village on its hill above the bay: it is like a secret fold in the earth, inviolate. We pitch Tiziana's tent in a big, dry glade with straw-colored fields all around its perimeter, a kilometer from the sea. The pine needles and brown, brittle eucalyptus leaves are soft underfoot. We tie a length of rope between two trees as a washing line. We spread a sheet on the floor of the tent to sleep on. There is a shower block, and a little café that sells *cappuccino* and *cornetti* for a euro.

The pine trees in the dunes have umbrella-shaped tops with dark, spur-like branches: their trunks are as thick and tall and fantastical as giants' legs. Pliny, from his naval vessel in the Bay of Naples, observed that the cloud given off by Vesuvius at its eruption was precisely the shape of an umbrella pine. These trees are ubiquitous in Italy: it is strange that the volcano should mirror their shape, as though a country could have a family of forms, just as it has a distinct language and race of people. The floor of the pinewood is soft and springy: it is undulating, mounded, primitive in appearance. There are people here. They walk soundlessly through the shade with its intricate stencils of light. They tread the narrow paths down to the beach and the sea. The water beats and heaves softly beyond the screen of trees. We follow a path that winds among the giant trunks. We are barefoot, brown-skinned, unburdened. The children carry their swimming towels in a roll under the arm. We have water, and a small secondhand hardback edition of Shakespeare's plays. We have a home six feet wide made of faded blue cloth, and a washing line. There seems to be no need for anything else. The bay is so warm, so soft, so simple: it

releases us from need, like sleep. Is it better to sleep than to need?
What was its purpose, all that need, the machinelike complexity of
our life at home, the desire for escape that was its dark emission?
A warm wind soughs through the pinewood and stirs the high-
up branches of the trees. In the distance we can see the humped
brown shapes of the Etruscan tombs. Then we come out into the
blinding light of the beach, the sand strewn with matted foliage,
the water rolling in its frill of surf. The countryside is rough, care-

free, running down to the edge of the sand. There are people
dotted about. They seem small, indistinct, both vague and multi-
farious, like forms etched by centuries of tides.

Our copy of Shakespeare has illustrations. They are highly
colored, artificial, like stills from an old Hollywood movie. There
is a drawing of Julius Caesar in his toga and laurel wreath, craggy
and superstitious-looking, his eyes sliding to the side. There is
Hamlet, black-clad and thin as a spider, with fair foppish hair.
They are realities become characters become realities again. I
brought the book to the beach with the intention of reading it myself, but the others want to read it too. The children do not run to
the rolling water, nor play in the earthy sand. Instead they sit one
on either side of me, their mouths by my ears, trying to see over
my shoulder. They want to know about Shakespeare. They want
to know the plot of *Othello*, of *Antony and Cleopatra*. They point to
things and ask what they mean. Every time I turn the page, they
complain. After a while I surrender and read aloud. I read them
Hamlet's soliloquies and Antony's love speeches and Macbeth's
unsettling remarks on the death of his wife. I do all three witches
in different voices. I do *The Tempest*, explaining as I go along.

The afternoon passes. A man comes up the beach selling slabs
of frozen pineapple. Later he comes back again, selling lemon
granite. People come and go through the heat haze, in and out of
the silent pinewoods. The sun begins to dip; slowly light leaves the
bay. The sea is milky, thick, mineral-colored. Evening approaches,
a blue-gray aura that stands on the hills and fields, as though
it has risen from the earth. The tombs cast shadows across the
grass. The sun sinks, bloodying the sky. It leaves behind it a feeling of weightlessness, of consciousness desisting. Everything is still,
trancelike. The water laps faintly at the shore. There are no lights
around the bay; the human day is barely marked. A month might

have passed, or a century. We roll up our towels and return to our tent. There are other tents in our glade; people are rinsing out their swimming costumes, heating things on little stoves, reorganizing their pots and pans. They do not relinquish their grip on time. They are standing up for civilization. In the tent next door there is a young German couple, fair and big-boned, who have prepared a hot meal for themselves and are sitting eating it at their folding table, where the glasses and cutlery and pepper pot have been nicely laid out. The girl serves the food to the boy, who sits upright and expectant in his chair. They are so young and yet so proper: I don't know whether to admire them or feel concerned on their behalf. How rigid and upright they are, how thoroughly disciplined, in this wild bay with its fields of ancient tombs, its giant primeval trees, its centuries that pass in an afternoon. They haven't turned up here with a volume of Shakespeare, a sheet, and a two-man tent that must somehow accommodate four. They have inflatable mattresses, which I watch the boy pump up after supper.

The children are playing *Hamlet*. One of them is Ophelia; the other is the prince. They have wrapped themselves in swimming towels tied at the shoulder, like togas. Come here Ophelia! commands the prince. Ophelia declines. I don't like you anymore, she says. Hamlet says that he's going to tell his mother. Fine, says Ophelia, disgustedly. Later Ophelia is discovered lying flat on her back in the pine needles. Help! she says, I can't swim! Hamlet is beside himself. He claws the floor of the glade in despair. Afterward he decorates her recumbent form with dead eucalyptus leaves.

We go to a little restaurant in the dark fields near the bay, where they give us *frito misto* in paper cones and Greco di Tufo wine, pale and chilled as an icicle. We walk on the beach in the spectral silver light of the sea. We cram into Tiziana's tent. It isn't

so bad. Its insubstantiality is strangely gratifying, for it makes manifest our determination to economize. The pitch costs fifteen euros
a night. Our boat back to England is booked for nine days hence.
I wonder whether we could stay here until the day before, and
then drive nonstop to Dieppe. I make pillows for the children out
of folded-up clothes. They put on their pajamas in the dark. It is
so hot that they don't want any covers. We have no torch: there will
be no reading. Instead I tell them the story of *Twelfth Night*.

∞

The next day we walk to the end of the bay, where there is a little
settlement of low white cottages, and a jetty with a handful of fish-
ing boats tethered along its side. In the shallows, a group of old
women sit playing cards. Their chairs and card table stand in six
inches of water, and they swirl their veined, swollen feet abstractedly in the clear sea while they play. The waves are just ripples
here, long, fine curves of silver that peal soundlessly one after another onto the sand, but sometimes a bigger wave comes, and the
women lift up their skirts and laugh.

We walk past the cottages and along a path that leads around
the rocks at the head of the bay. The rocks are flat and white: the
sea is turquoise-colored here, and so clear that the bottom of the
deep, shelving white valley of rock with its darting fish and fine,
fern-like plants can be seen from the edge. The water in the bay is
warm, and brown with leaves and matted balls of needles from the
pinewoods, but here there are sea urchins, blood-colored, like ru-
bies on the white rocks. The underwater valley looks as cool and
mysterious as if it were made of glass. Sunlight hangs in liquid
shapes above its crenellated ledges. It is hot, out here on the headland. There is nothing here. There is no shade. We scrutinize the

rocks where they meet the water, trying to establish a way in. We would have to jump, right over the sea urchins that encrust the shore and into the deeper section, where the fish move far below, winding through clear columns of shadow and light.

The children are nervous. They do not want to jump. The sea urchins frighten them. They have an instinctive terror of nacreous bodies that wait, unseen, in the water; of stings administered silently and without warning. It has taken them so long to establish that the world is predictable, that its elements are fixed, that its properties interrelate reliably: they will not easily forget their fear of the unknown.

I take a few steps back, and then run forward and hurl myself into the water. It was easy: I am in the deep part, swimming with the fish in regions of exquisite turquoise coolness. I tread water and look back to shore. Ophelia is having none of it. She has withdrawn from the waterside, and is sitting on a rock with her chin in her hands. But Hamlet is tempted. She stands on the brink, in an agony of indecision. She is a daredevil: she cannot bear to feel afraid, and so she is inexorably drawn to do the things she fears the most. I admire her for this trait, which I conspicuously lack, but I have failed to understand its significance, which is that she experiences more than the common portion of terror, not less. She is more frightened than Ophelia of jumping into the water, and for this reason she will force herself to do it, while Ophelia sits calmly on her rock. Her father tells her not to try: he thinks it is too dangerous after all. It was easy enough jumping in, but it is unclear how we are going to get out. But it is too late; Hamlet comes flying through the air, her fists clenched into balls at her sides, and thuds into the water beside me. She springs up again, victorious. For a while we swim around, but there is nowhere to put our feet. The water is deep here. I begin to see the difficulty. We swim toward the rocks and through the crystalline water Hamlet sees the sea urchins, plump and glossy as blood clots, as if through a magnifying glass. The game is up: there in the water she flings her arms around my neck and sticks there like a limpet. She is heavy and I thrash about, trying to stay afloat. I ask her to let go and she shrieks and tightens her grip. On her rock, Ophelia begins to cry. I realize that one way or another I am going to have to get us out.

I reach the rocks with Hamlet around my neck. Ophelia's crying is getting on my nerves. There is only one way back to the shore, which is to clamber up the shelving rock among the sea urchins. From a distance the rock looks smooth but close up it is chaotic and sharp. I cut my hands and feet, and so does Hamlet. We stagger out into the dry afternoon with its high white sun. Hamlet and Ophelia cry uncontrollably. I am angry. I don't know why, but I am angrier than I have ever been. I shout at them while blood runs down my legs. There are one or two Italians nearby, sunning themselves on the rocks. They look at us in consternation. They look at me. They know that the whole thing was entirely my fault. I am ashamed. I try to stop shouting but I can't. I can't.

∽

We roam in the soughing pinewoods. We lie by the water, talking. We peer at the Etruscan tombs, following dusty paths through fields of dry grass. There is the Tomb of the Chariots and the Tomb of the Attic Vases and the Tomb of the Funereal Couches. There are dome-shaped tombs like dirt-colored igloos in the grass. We stare at them but we do not understand them: they are the core, the impenetrable kernel of this land's mystery.

For four nights we sleep in the tent on its dry, rustling carpet of leaves. The children sleep deeply, soundlessly. We lie close together. In the darkness there is no perspective. It is like being held in the palm of a hand.

All day and all night I am half asleep and half awake. I am thinking about the future, though these thoughts are wordless and indistinct. They are like running water, a single entity. They pour toward an edge, a precipice, and tumble over the side. I do not want to go home. More precisely, I don't know *how* to go home. My consciousness runs swiftly, smoothly toward this edge and then tumbles over, a cataract. I need to find a path down out of these months in Italy. They stand behind us like mountains. To have climbed them, to have known their paths and peaks: in certain lights it has seemed that these are the dimensions of life itself, but lying in the tent I know this isn't so. Life could become flat again, ordinary again. It is desire that is big and grand and treacherous; desire, not life. I remember the Apuan mountains, their abysses, their glinting white fastnesses of rock: we will pass them on the road home and look up from the flatlands at their awful faces. We will remember that we were once there. But we will pass them. We will stay on the road.

A big group of Italian teenagers arrives, and they pitch their tents around ours in a circle. They giggle and shriek and sing English pop songs all night. Our clothes are filthy; there is nowhere to sit, except on the ground. Our hair is matted and our tent is full of ants. We wake up on the fifth day and realize that we want to leave Baratti. We pack up the car, and follow this slender thread of desire north.

∝

On the road outside La Spezia, the telephone rings. I have made some money: a South Korean publisher has bought the rights to one of my books, for a handsome sum. We cheer the South Koreans, zigzagging madly across both lanes of the N1. It is late afternoon, thirty-nine degrees, the sky gray and turbid and pregnant-looking. We turn off at Rapallo, looking for campsites. The road is dense with traffic. We crawl into town and out the other side, and follow the road down the Portofino peninsula. It does not seem likely that we will find a campsite along this road: the hills rise in steep green terraces to the right, and to the left plunge straight down to the sea. On the other side, back toward Rapallo, the cars have come to a standstill. The sky is clear here, and the sun is hot. A few people are getting out, to sit in the shade by the side of the road and wait. The rest keep their engines running and their tinted windows tight shut. Their forms can be glimpsed in the dark, air-conditioned interiors: they are like nocturnal animals, carved out of shadow, with strange glimmering accents embedded in their eyes and jewelry. There are some very expensive cars in the traffic jam. This is the rich Portofino crowd, whose giant yachts we see later in the harbor, dwarfing the narrow sunset-colored terraces. But the peninsula is beautiful, as lush and romantic as a Giorgione landscape, with its faded pink *palazzi*, its villas sunk in the trees, its road winding above the water. The cars form a little packed rope of anxiety, weaving through the loveliness of a dream.

It is past six o'clock and the children are hot and fretful. The dust of Baratti is everywhere, in our clothes and hair, caked in our nails. There is no turning back: the road the other way is at a standstill. We are being forced along the peninsula like something being digested. We inch toward Santa Margherita, and when we get there we abandon the car and walk in search of a hotel. The cheap hotels are full. The expensive hotels are full too. We try the ugly hotels: I feel sure that in Italy the ugly hotels will always have space. Up a backstreet I find a hotel that is situated in the middle of a concrete multistory car park. The receptionist is sitting in a glass box in a gray-carpeted foyer, from where long, low-ceilinged gray corridors with rows of identical doors extend out to every side. Through the foyer window, five or six feet away, I can see cars going up and down the concrete ramps of the car park: that is the only view. No other human being is visible, except for the receptionist in her box. She wears a red uniform, like an air hostess. She speaks to me through a grille. She tells me that the hotel is completely full.

We jump back in the car and reenter the traffic jam. It is dusk now, and the streets of Santa Margherita are full of people. They sit in the cafés with beautiful exquisite drinks, and walk freely out along the harbor in the sea breezes and rose-colored light. We gaze at them, parched and disconsolate. We have no choice but to go forward: the road back is paralyzed. We crawl out of the harbor and along the coast. It takes twenty minutes to go a hundred meters. The sea softly rises and falls beside us, pink and blue; far out on the water, a boat catches the last gold of the sun on its ivory sail. We shuffle on, impacted in our metal box. In front of us the road curves round out of sight: we strain impatiently to see what will be there. At last, tortuously, it discloses itself, a wooded bay, with a great white edifice standing above the water in a sweep of green lawns. It is so white, so sparkling: it is like the palace of some fabulous neurasthenic billionaire. A driveway rises to the porticoed entrance, and at the end of the driveway there is a magnificent pair of gates, with a brass plaque reading *Grand Hotel Miramare*. A man in a cap and white uniform is standing by the gates. We look at him, and he looks at us. He smiles, and gives a slight bow. As if of its own volition the car leaves the road, slewing right, barging through the traffic, past the brass plaque and up through the gates into the perfumed chirruping gardens, where it pauses to allow the uniformed man to lay his white-gloved hand gently on the rim of the filthy window. He is sure there will be a room available. When we are ready he will take our car to the hotel car park. If we indicate what luggage we require for the night, the porters will take it directly from the car to our room.

He wishes us a most pleasant evening at the Grand Hotel Miramare.

∽

The porters handle our noxious bags with rigorous politeness. No one looks at our feet, our clothes, our hair. The man at the desk offers us a suite: it is all he has left. We ask if he couldn't possibly find us something cheaper. No, no, he says, this suite is positively the only room free in the hotel tonight. He considers its freeness, there in front of us: perhaps, after all, this suite is something unwanted, passed over, like a woman past her prime. And here we are, late in the day, a match. It is past seven o'clock in the evening. As the suite remains unwanted, he will give it to us half price.

Our suite has a balcony facing the sea. In the white-tiled bathroom with its gold-plated taps we confer. We examine our luck, the snowy towels and bathrobes, the slippers with the hotel's name stitched across the toe, the miniature gold-capped bottles of bubble bath. We lie on the firm, enormous beds. Beneath our balcony, in the garden, there is a swimming pool. It is surrounded by lawns, and beyond them, the sea. We run downstairs and jump in, in the last light. There have been so many arrivals, so many cycles of desire and satisfaction, mounting and mounting through hours of chaos and uncertainty, building like a wave and then breaking, foaming with completion. Here is another: the empty oval of water that lies in the thick gray and violet dusk, the deserted lawns falling into darkness, the pale, quiet sea. A gardener in uniform moves among the shrubberies with their hedges and ornamental trees. Their forms are sculptural, abstract, hewn from big blocks of shadow. The man is indistinct, moving among the shadowy forms. He is less clear, less substantial than they. We jump into the water.

It is salty, and dark in its depths. We break its membrane: we send furrows and folds traveling across its surface. The light has nearly gone. The children swim away into darkness. They leave a wake behind them, a path of ripples that is a kind of memory of themselves, a record etched in the water. Their small heads make two round, black, dense shapes in the distances of the pool. Behind them the path erases itself: this is how they will live, advancing themselves through the yielding, unremembering world, holding their heads upright above the surface. It is half terrible, that they should have to support the mystery of their own selves, just as a work of art must support its own mystery and bear its own fate, however beautiful and beloved it is. For it seems so relentless to me there in the water, the erasing, the dissolving, the rubbing out of each minute by the next. Almost, it is unbearable. It strikes me that the glory of art is the glory of survival, for survival is an inhuman property. It is an attribute of mountains and objects, of the worthless toys in the children's bedroom at home that will outlive us all. That which is human decays and disappears: only in art does the quality of humanity favor survival. Only in art is a record kept of an instant, that the next instant doesn't erase.

The sky is steadily filling with cloud: it moves over the peninsula in a body, vast, like a dark glacier. For a while it builds around the bay, forming great cliffs at its edges that are gilded with paleness by the moon. Then the moon is engulfed and the cloud spreads out over the water. We get out and run back upstairs in our towels. Waiters are setting out dishes of nuts and olives in the hotel bar; the restaurant has lit its chandeliers, which blaze above the waiting tables. We dart up the grand marble staircase and along a corridor as wide as a boulevard to our room. But we meet no other guests; there is no one to shock with our attire, our dripping hair. And later, when we come down again, the blazing restaurant is still empty; the olives still sit mounded in their dishes. We do not intend to eat in the restaurant: a leather-bound menu on a gold plinth beside the door discloses the prices. But we stand there nonetheless, gazing through the doorway at the spectacle of its deserted grandeur, its inexplicable readiness, with its sparkling silver and crystal, its thick white napkins folded into pyramids, its tablecloths and fancy-backed chairs, for an event that seems to hover just beyond the boundary of perception. It is as though a delegation of ghosts is expected, or as though the notion of wealth itself is tonight to be honored and served, by the proud waiters who move among the tables making minute adjustments to the position of a glass or a fork.

Outside a warm wind is blowing. The sea is a field of dark inflections; the boats rock sleepily on their moorings. We walk along the road, into Santa Margherita, and find a table at a packed little place by the port, where the heat and laughter and the smells of cooking, the deep wooden shelves of beautiful wines, the baskets of rough bread, the old *padrone* in his stained apron, the faded color photographs of Italian landscapes, the glass cases of lemon tart and *tiramisù*, seem to distill all our manifold experiences into themselves; to become representative, even of things that bear no resemblance to them. Here are our travels, transitory but alive; here, again, is the reality, the moment that breaks and foams. We will not always live like this. We are going home, to work, to settle down, to send the children to school. Later, their teacher is discomposed by their lack of familiarity with the conventions of the classroom. They have forgotten their maths, or perhaps it is merely that they have forgotten their place among their peers. They have forgotten how to live anywhere but at the center of experience. Everything that now seems so real will soon be suspended; soon, the other reality will be unwrapped and reassembled. They are so dif-

ferent, these two realities. The first is the reality of the moment, of
the sky as it looks tonight over Santa Margherita, of the *spaghetti
alle vongole* and the satirical face of the *padrone* and the eczematic re-
production of Leonardo's *Last Supper* that hangs in a cheap gilded
frame beside our table. And the other: what is the other?

Beyond the steamed-up windows the storm breaks over the
port. The water rushes down, hurling itself on the paving stones.
It cascades off the awnings and runs in brown rivers along the gut-

ters. Walking home, we are soaked to the skin, but later, standing on our balcony, we watch branches of lightning illuminate the tossing surface of the sea, jagged paths of electricity that struggle briefly to find some route into the earth, and in their failure brilliantly expend themselves and are extinguished.

∝

The children have made two friends: we go out to breakfast on the hotel terrace to discover that they have affianced themselves to the daughters of an American millionaire with a pockmarked face and small blue eyes that look wearily at something over your shoulder. The Americans are at the Miramare for a fortnight, and our children are the first playmates they have found since their arrival a week earlier. The mother comes across to look us over. She is tall, powerfully built, with a slouching, cowboyish gait; but she is strangely pale and flaccid-looking. She too has a weary, offhand demeanor: she stands beside her husband and the two of them tell us about their tour of Europe, reeling off a list of countries and capital cities with a striking lack of animation, so that Paris and Prague seem to deflate a little before our eyes. We are still struggling to digest the notion of two whole weeks at the Grand Hotel Miramare. What strange, inexplicable luxury! The sun is shining once more: the other guests have come out for breakfast on the terrace. There are one or two bejeweled old ladies with tiny, fretful dogs, but otherwise they do not compose a particular type. They are all different, and they are all rich. The American woman does display a minor inconsistency: unlike the others, her clothes look as though she has worn them at least once before.

The children want to go to the beach club—their new friends have told them all about it. Apparently, the hotel has a private beach, directly below. This is where the Americans have been spending their days. The two sets of children cling onto one another, as though we might attempt to tear them asunder. The Americans have been on the road almost as long as we have, far from the society of other English-speaking children, and all four girls have the hunger of émigrés for the forsaken world, the world of friendship. It is as though they have encountered fellow citizens from the homeland, the old country. Girls their own age! A whole familiar, vanished way of life is suddenly present to them once more, with its particular references and language and atmosphere. They want to speak it, this language; they want to reminisce; they want to go to the beach club.

The Americans ask when we are leaving. Earlier, the man at the desk told us gravely that we were free to stay all day and make use of every hotel facility, but this offering does not satisfy the Americans. I watch them weigh it up, the day and its profits: they had been planning to go to Portofino for lunch. It is not a sound investment, their relationship with us. There are no long-term dividends. They are disappointed, almost angry. Our stock has no value: a measly day is all it's worth. The father is inclined to jettison us straightaway. He wants to go to Portofino, as agreed. Instantly his daughters are distraught, almost tearful: they have a white, strained look about them that causes my own children to fall silent and gaze at them anxiously. The mother speaks. She is unemotional: she seems to stand in great desolate prairies of neutrality. She says that they will go to Portofino later, at four o'clock. Until then, the girls are free to be at the beach club. At four o'clock she will expect them to come without being told. She herself is going to go and lie down. She goes, and we are left with the father. There is only one thing for it: we offer to take charge of the children, and return them to the hotel at four. He nods curtly. He has got a good deal after all. Desire has been swabbed away from him: spongelike, we have absorbed the embarrassment of the whole situation. He walks slowly back to his table and picks up his copy of the *Herald Tribune*.

At the beach club there is a marine trampoline, riding out on the waves. The sea is ebullient, after the storm. All day the children swim out, and are dashed deliriously back onto the beach. They bounce madly on the trampoline. They have funny conversations, which I overhear in fragments from behind the cover of my book. The Americans have a friend in England called Sophie. Do we know her? I hear my daughter talking about her best friend Milly. Do they know Milly? She's so nice.

Later I hear the American girls talking about their mother. She's really sick, the older one says. I sit up: I want to explain to my daughters what that means. I want them to be kind. They are sitting in a row on the shoreline in their swimming costumes. Sometimes a wave comes up and foams at their feet. They are tossing pebbles into the water. I buy them an ice cream. I leave them be.

THE LAST SUPPER

At Ventimiglia, near the French border, we turn off the coast road and drive up into the hills. We are looking for somewhere to pitch Tiziana's tent. It is six o'clock, still hot. The countryside is a little ragged, scarred here and there with enterprise, and with the formlessness of frontier places where the feeling of identity comes in unpredictable surges and then frays again, like an unraveling hem. The road goes up and up. We pass parked lorries and derelict roadside restaurants, travel through villages that cling along the verges and then peter out. The irresolute green vista resumes hesitantly, after each pause. We reach Dolceacqua and the broad brown Nervia River. There is a feeling here of civilization and abandonment, of something dead that was once alive: the ruined castle on its hill, the ancient arc of the great stone bridge, the tall, narrow, ravaged-looking terraces. Everywhere there are vineyards, modernized, bristling with signs. We stop and ask the way to the campsite, and are directed on ahead.

At last the campsite appears, a modest roadside place in its obscurity of low hills, where nonetheless there are people, established in their dusty pitches beneath the trees as though they had lived there all their lives. There are some mobile homes, where washing hangs on lines and television sets flicker through the windows. There are Dutch tents and German tents and tiny podlike tents with bicycles parked outside. There is a little bar and a café, and next to that a small rectangular swimming pool. The sky is overcast and gray: the dingy pool is full of children, whose parents sit in white plastic chairs on the concrete tiles. It is slightly desolate, this arrangement, though everyone seems to accept it. The countryside extends indifferently around; the sky is moody overhead; the parents lie torpid in their chairs, or rouse themselves to sudden, startling fits of activity, plunging heavily in and hurling their offspring shrieking across the water. Shortly after we arrive, everyone abandons the swimming pool and returns to their tents. It is no longer hot, but we will swim in any case. In the traffic jams of Ventimiglia, where we crawled through the dusty, constricted streets of the *città vecchia* behind giant lorries bound for Nice and Marseilles, the sun was cruel and adversarial, faintly humiliating: it was a form of oppression, from which swimming offered the only possibility of liberation. But we could find no road down to the sea at Ventimiglia, and in the end the heat passed, undefied. We defy it now, in retrospect, circulating around the cloudy water where children's blow-up toys drift, forgotten, across the surface beneath the gray sky. Desire and satisfaction have become uncoupled. There will be no consummation tonight. There will be no resolution, no declaration of the day's victory, no enshrining of its significance. We have reentered the other reality. We have returned to the ordinary, unexamined experience of life.

We pitch our tent on a dirt terrace in the trees, between two other tents. Everything is silent. People walk to and fro, commuting to the sinks and the shower block. Their flip-flops slap against the soles of their feet as they pass. They carry wash bags, dirty dishes, boxes of detergent. They glance at us beside our tent. When we ourselves walk to the shower block, the people by their tents glance at us. It has grown dark, though we were not aware of the sun setting. The light drained unremarked from the wadded sky with its screen of hills, and left behind an arid darkness. We go to the bar, which is empty. After a while a man comes through, and we ask if there is anything to eat. He thinks there is not. He says that he will go and talk to his wife. The wife appears: they are not serving food, but she has cooked *spaghetti alla bolognese* for herself and her husband. If we think that will be satisfactory, then we are welcome to share it. She will serve it on the terrace by the swimming pool, with a bottle of wine from their vineyard.

We go out and sit on the terrace. There is no one there. The sky is full of stars. The pool is inky, inchoate, flecked with silver. It has soothed us, this encounter with the man and his wife, but it has aroused our emotions too. It has awoken our love for Italy just as we had entered the gray prospect of leaving it. We are nervous, a little shaky. We discuss our plans, the two nights that remain after this one before we catch the boat. I want to stay here, on this side of the border. I don't care what the campsite is like. I don't want to leave. The children run around in the dark. The woman brings our food in a big silver covered dish. She is worried it will not be enough, but when she takes off the cover we see that there is almost more than we can eat. Later the husband comes out to see how we are getting on, and when we praise the spaghetti he becomes eloquent, descanting gently in the starlight on the glories of his wife's cooking as he clears the plates. This was our last supper: it was difficult to recognize it, to understand it, until it was complete. We go to our tent, and lie listening to dogs barking somewhere in the valley.

The next day we find ourselves in Dolceacqua, wandering aimlessly through its dark viscera of alleyways, where tiny doors lead up to dwellings of unimaginable exigence and dilapidation. In the sloping, deserted, pockmarked piazza the church bell is tolling. Through an open window high up in a crevice-like street I hear someone playing a song by The Cure. The river runs between its dry, dusty banks. We climb up to the ruined castle and stare into its blackened interior. Coming down, we take the wrong path and find ourselves in a car park surrounded by wire fences. It is too hot to go back up. We pass through a gap in the fence and down a steep, narrow stairway that twists and twists across a derelict, litter-strewn hillside. It leads to a kind of catacomb beneath the village, a dank network of tunnels and passages where we stoop beneath the low ceilings, searching for a way out. Suddenly we are tired of being here. Here is where we neither want nor have to be. It is one or the other, duty or desire, freedom or responsibility. That is the pendulum swing, the inescapable arc of life. But this place we have the power to leave.

We go back and pack up the tent. The pool is full of children again. Their parents sit prostrated in their white plastic chairs. There is the sound of splashing water, and of people calling to one another in German. At four o'clock we are on the road down to Ventimiglia. We take the exit to Nice, fly through a checkpoint where a traffic policeman in a beautiful uniform waves us on with his white gloves, and enter a tunnel that passes straight through a hillside into France. We come out, blinking, in the bleached light of the Côte d'Azur. It is strange, that the violence of leaving Italy should occur without sensation. It was a single blow, swift and numbing, virtually painless. But when we stop to get petrol and water outside Nice, I feel a nameless sense of bereavement. The French words are uncomfortable in my mouth. The girl behind the till is busy, distracted, sullen. I stand before her; I feel that I have something in my hands, something large and shimmering and important, something I am aching to give. There are people behind me in the queue. They are impatient; this is a big place on a hot motorway where needs are processed without sentiment. But sentiment is what I require; I require feeling, acknowledgment, kindness. I ask whether they sell road maps—we have lost ours. She doesn't hear me, so I ask again. This time she understands. She is incredulous, disgusted: it is outrageous, that I have asked her such a question. It is as if I have robbed her of something. I am struck by the economy of her outrage. It takes a second, no more. She points to the shelves. Go and look, she says.

∝

We can't find a place to camp. We drive around the empty French countryside. It is late afternoon, the sky still and gray, torpid. Everything seems stunned, anesthetized. We pass a place where little white houses made of corrugated tin rise in rows up a denuded hillside. It is a holiday park. The man tells us they have an area for tents. He is tall and broad and ruddy, like a farmer, but one of his arms dangles shrunken and deformed from his shirtsleeve.

We go into his office, a wooden cabin that stands on a circle of gravel. He writes down our details using his good arm. While we are standing there a family come in. They are Dutch, a well-dressed couple and two fair-haired children. The father instantly starts to shout. He shouts in English. He is shouting at the top of his voice, at the manager of the holiday park, who continues carefully writing. After an interval, the manager looks up. The Dutchman is beside himself: cords of muscle stand out around his neck, and his pale eyes look as though they might fly out of their sockets. He is still shouting: his wife ushers their children outside. He shouts that they have been tricked, deceived, misled. The manager is a villain, a liar. They have come here all the way from Holland, all the way here for a two-week sojourn at the holiday park, and what do they find? I pay attention: I am interested to know what they have found. Despite his aggressive manner, I am even a little sympathetic. I expect him to say that what they found was a dump full of tin huts, instead of the Provençal idyll doubtlessly advertised. But he does not say that. He barks his accusation with a mouth rectangular with rage, like a letterbox. Its substance is that they have been given a different tin hut from the tin hut they booked at home, on the Internet. But *monsieur*, the manager says with a shrug, the huts are all the same. At this the Dutchman screams. *I refer to the position of the hut! The position of the hut is inferior!* A fusillade of expletives issues from his mouth. Suddenly I am afraid for the manager. I think the Dutchman is going to kill him. His anger is delinquent, bizarre. He is a narrow, colorless man, a suit. The manager, with his deformity, seems like someone he might choose as a victim. The manager rises from his chair: he is twice the Dutchman's size. But he is somehow broken, wounded. He doesn't seem to care whether the Dutchman kills him or not. He has a withered arm; his holiday park *is* a dump. It would almost be better if that was what the Dutchman was angry about. He tells him to wait; he is going to show us where to put our tent. When he returns, he will see if he can rectify the problem. The Dutchman immediately stalks out of the cabin. Later we see him, standing on the gravel with his family. He is very upright, rigid, as though with the shock of his own significance. His face is white. He has a puny, triumphant air: he has been fobbed off, but he is telling himself that he acted like a man.

We follow the manager up a dirt road that zigzags interminably through the white tin suburb and then comes out at the top on a stony ledge. The stony ledge is where we are permitted to pitch our tent. It is too late to argue: we put the tent up and get back in the car. It is nearly dark, and we need to find something to eat. There is a village a few kilometers away. When we get there we are surprised to find that it is packed with people. The center is completely closed off. We park the car and walk. In the square a giant screen has been put up, and the buildings are all strung with flags. It is the World Cup final: France are playing Italy. The square is crowded, with old ladies and children, with gangs of kohl-eyed teenagers in black drainpipes and plump middle-aged couples. Everywhere there are shirtsleeved delegations of men locked in endless, cheerful conference.

We find a seat, get beer and food from a stall. We feel a little treacherous, though our treachery is all against Italy. It is not this prosperous French village we are deceiving: we are sure that France will win. They *have* to win, for much the same reason that we had to leave Italy—because reality requires it. Anything else would be fantastical, improvident. The French have Zidane, rationality, form. These are the things on which expectations can be based and decisions reached. What do the Italians have? I remember the traffic policeman who stood at the mouth of the tunnel with his elaborate braided uniform, his long leather boots, his snowy gloves, his manner that was both theatrical and sincere. He courteously waved us out of his land like an actor at the final curtain. The Italians have splendor. What would a decision be like that had splendor as its basis? To what strange, beautiful expectations would it give rise?

The French do not win the World Cup final. The Italians win. Zidane assaults one of the Italian players, butting him with his white, domed, rational forehead. We return to the rocky ledge, where all night the hard, uneven ground probes our slumber and sends our bodies roaming around the tent, searching for flat places, for relief.

∝

The fields of the Charente are yellow, with chalky white partings like hair. Grain silos stand in their flat distances: they are gray, concrete, shaped like giant hourglasses. Their swollen forms are dominating, implacable. They stand upright between the horizontal planes of field and sky, alone, as though they had devoured everything that was once there.

We come off the motorway at St. Jean d'Angély and skim through the silent, yellow-white landscape. The road is completely straight: it stretches on for as far as the eye can see, pale gray and empty. The children gaze through the open windows. They are very quiet. Now and again a straight line of trees passes, at right angles to the road, and their eyes flicker, mathematically registering the perspective. We have booked a room in a hotel: we arranged it by phone. Tiziana's tent has been folded into its bag. It is our last night before England, a night for reflection, order, readiness. The world is once more flat and straight, symmetrical. It is bare and clean, blank, like paper. It seems to invite something, some final utterance. What can we say, to the blank yellow-white fields? What should we inscribe along the straight lines of trees?

We follow our directions: at a junction where four narrow white roads depart in four different directions across the flat fields, and where a few stone houses stand at the crossroads displaying pots of red geraniums but no people, we turn left. The road goes straight, into the yellow distances. Now and again there is a right angle, and then a straight section, and then another right angle. We are driving around the perimeters of fields. Sometimes we pass a small white house, sitting behind its fence. After a while we come to a dip, a kind of ripple in the earth. The lines of trees go down and come up again. The expanse of yellow grain describes it with its level, brushlike fibers, this perfect concavity. It falls and rises; it rolls like the sea. How strange and mysterious the world is, describing itself with such rigorous perfection: it is as though description is its ambition, its only purpose. The road enters the dip, descends and comes up again. In front of us there is a screen of dark green trees. The light is chalky, faintly unreal. It gives a kind of flatness to everything, like paint; it describes them, the green trees and the white road, the undulating yellow field. We pass through a pair of stone gates and along a driveway of pale, fine dirt. At the end there is a house. It is a grand house, long and low, light gray, with two rows of shuttered windows. The white, bleaching light is full on its face. The glass in the windows is dark. It is like something someone is remembering. To the left there is a long stone building with high-up windows, like a barn. The terrain is so flat that nothing is visible beyond the screen of trees.

We get out of the car and knock at the door. After a while a girl opens it. She is twenty or so, fine-skinned and tousle-haired, cheerful. She has an air of casual sophistication, of groomed self-absorption, like someone who has returned for the holidays from her small, elite university. She shows us inside: her aunt is not here, she has gone shopping in St. Jean. She will be back in an hour. In the meantime she will show us to our rooms. She consults a vast ledger with yellowed pages that stands on a wooden bureau in the hall. She chews her clean fingernail: she is not entirely certain where her aunt intended to put us. She will go and ask Hélène. We will do her the kindness of waiting in the salon for a moment.

We pass through a doorway into a large, low-ceilinged room. It is dark: the shutters are closed against the afternoon sun. Seams of white light show around their edges. The room is full of furniture. There are antique dressers and cabinets, desks and ornamental tables, a grand piano, bookshelves with glass-fronted doors. On every surface there are great numbers of things: dancing china figurines, items made of bronze and silver and glass, bowls and boxes and lampstands, glass paperweights with tiny flowers imprisoned in their depths, goblets of colored crystal, tapestries and sprays of silk roses, sea chests full of old lace, clocks and bells and a music box beneath a glass dome, faded photographs, tea sets, books with threadbare spines, hats and tiny pairs of pearl-buttoned gloves, and in a corner a mannequin, an antique dressmaker's headless dummy with a rope of beads around her amputated neck. These things are not here by chance: there is no disorder, no element of chaos in this curious spectacle. Everything has been arranged, that much is clear. There is no dust on the dome of the music box; the velvet-upholstered chaise and chintz-covered armchairs are in their proper places in the gloom. There is no one sitting in them, but they have an atmosphere of animation. An invisible presence animates them. It is like a room in a doll's house: at any moment, it seems, a large hand could descend, pluck something from its place, and rearrange it, in order to further the game.

The girl returns. She has a woman with her, a smooth, rounded, thickset woman in her thirties, with sallow skin and fair hair in two thick plaits. She emanates a stormy kind of vitality. Her powerful eyes are long and dark and heavy-lidded; her mouth is large and plastic. She is like one of Picasso's colossal, Hellenic women who run by the blue water with uplifted arms. She looks at us, unsmiling. She speaks in a low voice to the girl. Then she vanishes again through the doorway.

We are led upstairs, up a creaking staircase and into a room with windows to the front and dark red wallpaper and a four-poster bed with white curtains. There is another room adjoining it; it is all perfectly pleasant. We thank the girl and she goes away. I sit on the bed. There is a book on the table beside it. I pick it up: it is a small paperback book, very old and faded. The spine crackles when I open it. It is in English. It is a handbook of advice issued by the War Office for soldiers departing for the Western Front. There is a man's name, written inside the front cover in ink, and a date, 1917. I read a section on the care and maintenance of your rifle and uniform in the trenches. I read about what to do if you encounter your enemy in the road. How will you know he is your enemy? I read instructions for bravery. How will you know how to be brave? To be brave, it is necessary to place a restraint on your self-love. Love has left few traces in this world. Instead: courage, honor, duty. Without love there would be no tragedy. That would be easier, would it not? One might deny the existence of love, for this reason. I look at the man's name again, at his handwriting. It is very sad, this book. Why has it been left beside my bed? There is something a little barbed, a little ironic, in its placement. It wishes, almost, to laugh at the quaintness of male valor. It wishes to conjure up the rigidity, the conservatism, the compliance of the male soul.

The children want to go out to the garden. There is a lawn, with winding paths and bushes and trees that mass and obscure one another, so that it is impossible to see where the garden ends. We go down, and out through a pair of glass doors. A warm, dry wind is blowing. I sit on the grass, and the children run away down the paths and disappear. I watch the tops of the trees, turning and bowing in the wind. I watch the grass, its dry shifting filaments electric in the sunlight. Suddenly I am cold: I feel a prickling of the skin, a sense of exposure. I go back upstairs to get a jacket. Passing the bed, I notice that the soldier book is no longer on the table. A different book is there. Someone has come in and changed it. It seems that I am being directed. I do not like being directed. I do not touch the book: I do not want to know what it is. The room is silent, full of white light. I get my jacket and quickly go back outside again. I sit on the grass, and then lie down, on my side. I am very tired. I close my eyes. The white light and the wind feel as though they are in my head. I only know that I have gone to sleep when the sound of a bell wakes me up. It is ringing in the garden, somewhere nearby. It is a handbell: it makes a loud, sonorous, clanging sound. I can hear a woman's voice calling. *Les enfants!* she shouts. *Les enfants!* I wonder which children she is calling: I haven't seen any here. I sit up, and observe the fair-haired woman with the strange eyes striding down toward the end of the garden. It is she who is ringing the bell, and calling. *Les enfants! La maison de jeux est ouverte! La maison de jeux est ouverte! Les enfants!* A while later she returns, with my daughters running behind her. They stop to speak to me. They are excited. They say that the lady is going to show them the house of games. She has walked on ahead and vanished through the glass doors. They run after her, and I get stiffly up to follow.

In the house, in the gloom of the salon, there is a woman. She is tall, erect, gray-haired. She has a broad, bare face that is full of creases. She has small, penetrating, merciless eyes. She holds out her hand to greet me. She is Madame, the mistress of this faintly unsettling domain. She is the third and, I can see, the most powerful of the household triumvirate. While she speaks, I calculate: she is the aunt of the young girl, and the mother of the saturnine Hélène, the fair-haired woman who was ringing the bell. I see that they are a caucus, a set. I compliment her on her house, her wondrous collection of *objets*, and she eyes me, smiling like a snake.

The children have gone to the *maison de jeux*, she says. My daughter has opened it for them.

I say that it is very kind of her: the children will be pleased to find some toys to play with. It is very sensible, I say, to have such a facility. It might stop them trying to play with her antiques.

They can touch whatever they like, she says, smiling, as long as they do not break it.

Unexpectedly, the children return. I hear them running down the hallway. They fly into the salon: their faces are strange. I ask if they have seen the house of games. Yes, they say. Why did they not stay there? They do not reply. Madame is looking at them. She wears an expression of cold amusement on her face. I sense that she is offended, or disappointed: I sense that they have failed. I take their hands and ask them to show it to me, and they lead me through the hall and out across the white light of the drive toward the barn. At the door, they stop. It's in there, they say. They do not want to come in. They have seen it already.

I go through the door, out of the white light. The barn is dark. There is music playing. It is piano music, Debussy, coming from somewhere in the middle of the large, open room. I am in a kind of tunnel of black draperies. I push my way through and find myself face-to-face with a mannequin. She is tall and flaxen-haired, and she wears a long sequined gown. For a moment I am startled: I thought she was real. Her hand is outstretched, fingers splayed, as though I might be expected to bend down and kiss them. But her eyes—her eyes are so large and liquid, so intricate in their irises, so filled with painted expression. In the end it is her hair that gives her away. She wears a beaded headdress with a blue feather stitched in the band, and her yellow synthetic hair curls stiffly around it. Beside her there is a wardrobe with its doors open. Inside there are many shelves. They are crammed with female finery, with delicate shoes and evening bags, with fans and feather boas and costume jewelry. It is a little sinister—it is a kind of mausoleum: there is something of the bureaucracy of death about the rows of old handbags, the neatly stacked pairs of worn shoes.

I move on, along the black-draped corridor. There are two more mannequins, a man and a woman. They are in wedding clothes: the woman wears a ruffled white dress with a big, bell-shaped skirt, and a veil in her hair. The man is in morning dress. They are arm in arm, looking ecstatically into each other's eyes. Next there is a whole scene, lit with bright electric stage lights. There are children, and a baby in a cradle. There is a little dog, and a cat playing with a ball of wool. It is a room in a family house: there is a man sitting in an armchair and a woman in an apron, and a table with a cloth and plates laid out. They are so

strange, so lifelike. They have such a touching air of mortality: they seem more mortal than people of flesh and blood. I pass a woman in silver lamé, two children ardently holding hands, an aviator with a stricken, ghastly face. Then more women, delicate, with tapered fingertips and fronded eyes, with slender necks and heads inclined, all clad in chiffon and satin and silk. They stand on every side, in attitudes of tragic modesty, so beautiful and forlorn;

and everywhere there are cupboards of clothes and hats and jewelry, gorgeous and redundant, in whose arc of possibility, of destiny, their frozen plastic forms are contained. It is their atom of
life, of art, that imprisons them. They are like painted women,
sealed in their instant of reality. Is it so brief, so fleeting, the moment of perception? How is the world to be comprehended, described, if instants are all there can be?

I turn a corner and there is the woman, Hélène, sitting on a
red velvet sofa. She has been waiting. She looks at me with her
strange, slanting eyes. Her face is defiant and vulnerable. She
reaches next to her to adjust the volume of the piano music. She
tells me that the *maison de jeux* is all her own work. She created it
herself, the whole spectacle. She has been collecting clothes and
mannequins since she was a child. Her mother allowed her to
use the barn: she made her first model when she was sixteen.
Since then it has been her life. She has always lived here, with her
mother. She has collected mannequins from many different periods, in order to demonstrate historical variations in the perception
of the female form. For her, women are the victims of perception.
In the mannequins she has found a new means of expressing the
reality of the female body.

I say that she has painted their eyes beautifully. It is incredible:
they almost seem to be alive.

She looks at me eerily. I see something in her expression, a
flash of lawlessness, almost of violence. I see the soul of the artist
open briefly before me like a chasm and disclose its dark and pa-
gan power.

I didn't paint their eyes, she says. They came with their eyes
like that. That is just how they are.

Outside the light is so strong that for a moment the world is all
white, bleached of its content. I call the children. I try to summon

them out of this emptiness. It is like the first stroke of the brush on a clean canvas: my voice, causative. In a minute they will come. I want them to. I want there to be something where now there is nothing.

Later, back in England, I often think of that place, of Hélène and her mother and the *maison de jeux*. Sometimes, though we have changed many things, our life at home takes on its old appearance of fixity and predetermination. I feel the old turbulence, the disunity with the actual. It is usually then, if I do remember her, that I will remember Hélène. I remember that I am not the victim of perception. I remember her air of combat, her awkwardness, her strange violent eyes. She recognized me, as I did her. Such moments are like paintings: they do not take much account of time. They pass straight through it. They sever its tangled fibers. They pass through the heart of an instant, on their way somewhere else.

CPSIA information can be obtained
at www.ICGtesting.com
Printed in the USA
LVOW03s1815030418

572145LV00001B/60/P